SAINT CAMILLUS

St. Camillus

by EDMUND F. CURLEY

THE BRUCE PUBLISHING COMPANY

MILWAUKEE

TO THE REVEREND PETER J. MCDONOUGH
PASTOR OF ST. JOHN THE EVANGELIST CHURCH
SWAMPSCOTT, MASSACHUSETTS
WITH AFFECTION FROM ALL THE CURLEYS

Library of Congress Catalog Card Number: 62–18225

FOREWORD

One of the great acts of altruism is the care of the sick. In today's world this is an accepted obligation of humanity. History, however, records dark days when our fellow beings in ill health were not only neglected but feared and shunned. There are many millions who believe the Red Cross, symbol of mercy and refuge of the stricken, came into existence during the past century. The world hails Florence Nightingale as the originator. The true founder of the Red Cross, worn on the cassocks of his followers for almost four hundred years, was one whose life is a striking example of God's influence upon a man of His choice.

This is the story of the early struggles of Camillus de Lellis and the final realization of his objective, the founding of a religious order devoted to the sick.

It is the true odyssey of a remarkable man. Soldier of fortune, inveterate gambler, drinker, brawler, wandering beggar, we also see him as the most Christian of men, a shining beacon in the progress of mankind, a true warrior in the Army of Christ, a saint of the Holy Catholic Church.

On his shoulders, for the first time in history, fell the mantle of the Red Cross in 1586.

SAINT CAMILLUS

CHAPTER I

In the Abruzzo district, northwest of Rome, the turreted walls of ancient fortified towns perched on the brink of green forested ravines and cast the shadows of a two thousand year old grandeur over the valleys. Foliage in all its shades, from the dark austerity of cypress to the silvery sheen of olive, stretched endlessly against a backdrop of multi-hued pallisades.

Bucchianico lay here, a dusty jewel in the hot summer of 1568. The August haze hung over the purple vineyards, over the pure emerald of fig trees and the scarlet and yellow tiled roofs of stone houses. It trailed tendrils that dropped to the glittering bosom of the tiny stream that edged the town. Blue mountains, smoky in the distance, ringed the picture.

The noonday burned hot but in the valley it was cool, except in the hearts of the simple peasantry where exasperation had finally reached the ultimate. A custom of untold lineage had been shattered, an unwritten rule for all inhabitants had been tossed to the wind. The quiet that always reigned in the town at midday was replaced by loud cries and imprecations rising above the scuffling of three youths in the dusty square at the back of the miller's warehouse.

Giovanni D'Allesandro, the miller, about to draw the shutters on the second floor, stared down at the circle of boys surrounding the brawlers. "Antonio," he called to his helper, "come quickly! That devil is at it again and I think he has met his match. The two against him are the Manetti twins. They will surely give him the beating he has asked for."

"Let me see." Antonio crowded into the window place.

"Ah, it is as you say. Look, there is a good one for him."

The trio of fighters were stripped to the waist. Two, short and powerful, faced the extremely tall yet well-proportioned form of another, upon whose face was a reddening mask of blood and rage. Even at a distance the two men noted the bared teeth and flaming eyes.

"I tell you he is certainly possessed," said Antonio.

"Let us hope that the Mannetti boys take good care of him," Giovanni replied with relish.

The noise from the onlookers was increasing as cries of encouragement broke out.

"Go in from each side, Luigi."

"Get him from front and back."

"Hold them in front of you, Camillus. Do not let them circle."

The tall youth was wary and watched his adversaries as they started to separate. He suddenly let out a wild yell and leaped at the one called Luigi. The sudden onslaught was met with a few blows that were completely disregarded. Luigi staggered from a return flailing and then felt arms of steel about him. He was lifted into the air and slammed to the ground just as his twin rushed to the rescue.

"Watch out, Camillus!" someone shouted to the tall one who met the onrush and proceeded to hammer at the other brother with a fury that could not be faced. His second opponent fell to the ground and then the victor took hold of both and dragged them together. He seized each under an arm and brought their heads together with a resounding crack, then threw them from him. They hit the earth and lay unconscious.

"He is the devil!" Giovanni shouted. "Here, you, Camillus de Lellis! Be off or I will have the police after you. You bully! You scoundrel!"

"Come down and I will give you some of the same, my fat miller." The tall youth was struggling with his shirt while others crowded about the bruised and fallen losers.

"Such impudence!" Antonio raved.

"I'll fix you, you devil!" Giovanni shouted.

"Fix your rotten flour and leave me alone." The victor made a gesture that further infuriated the merchant.

Some of the audience gathered about the winner voicing their congratulations. "It was nothing," was the reply, "They started the fight. I will have no one threaten me, least of all such scum as they." He stalked proudly from the dusty arena leaving the losers to the ministrations of their friends.

"That settles it!" Giovanni roared, pounding the window-sill. "I have had enough of that rascal's fighting and insults. No doubt he was half drunk."

"Well, it was two against one," Antonio said. "There is no doubt that he can fight."

"It is in his blood," the miller fumed. "I am going to see a few people in this town. We will soon find out if this eighteen-year-old villain is going to dominate the respectable citizens. He called me fat and called my flour rotten. I will not stand for this." Giovanni, thoroughly infuriated, forgot his time of rest and immediately set out on a round of visits to certain leaders in the little town.

Two hours later, Lorenzo the shoemaker, Rodrigo the armorer, Bianco the baker, and a dozen men of lesser worth crowded into the cool garden retreat of Father D'Agostino, the parish priest. The cleric, surprised, sensed trouble and insisted that they all sit before they spoke. "Now, my sons," he said gently, "what can I do for you?"

Giovanni started. "It is about Camillus de Lellis — "

"Ah!" It was not a new subject to the priest. He sat down and carefully looked at his visitors. "What is it now?"

Giovanni volunteered the information. "Today he beat the Manetti boys into unconsciousness. When I sought to stop him he heaped abuse upon me."

"Already the young men of the town talk of nothing but gaming and fighting," Lorenzo added. "It is all due to him."

"Our boys are swaggering bravos," said Bianco. "They do not wish to do any kind of work. My own son gambles like a Spaniard, games that I do not even know and all because of this devil."

"A harsh name, Bianco," said the priest.

"Have you anything good that can be said of him?" Rodrigo asked.

The priest held up his hand. "There is good, more good than bad in every man, for there is something of the Maker in all of us."

"Yet there are still evil men," Lorenzo said doggedly. "Camillus de Lellis has caused us enough woe. We have called on you to help, not to hear him defended."

"What do you wish me to do?"

"Tell him to leave us, to take his evil ways and habits and go, never to return."

"Who has authority to do that?"

Dismay was expressed on all their faces. Finally Bianco spoke. "Then it is a hopeless thing and he has become the curse and dread of all the town."

"I have known of his actions as well as you," Father D'Agostino said. "I have reprimanded him for his absence from Mass and the sacraments but there is still much good in him."

"What is this good that we cannot see?"

"Have any of your daughters suffered from him by the slightest word or action?"

The men were silent.

Rodrigo was the first to speak. "Yes, you are right there, Father. He has not that name, but you know that he drinks and gambles and will fight at the slightest chance, usually uncalled for. These things he loves."

"So there is still good in him. He has a nobility of soul. It is true that he has caused much trouble and it has been my intention to speak to him."

"He should be exorcised," Rodrigo said.

The priest smiled. "And who would hold him while I poured the holy water?"

"Can you tell us what to do?"

"I have news for you, my sons. When I came down the mountain road this morning from a sick visit I met a man who was riding into town."

"A man? What man?"

"One time captain of the garrison in this town and now at Pescara."

"Giovanni de Lellis! God will surely have to help us now."

"So he has come back."

"The town will have no rest."

"He is at his cousin's house," the priest said. "I was about to go there when you arrived. I intend to speak about this very matter."

"You have hopes, Father?"

"And courage, also?"

"I am never without hope, my sons. That is what we live upon. As for courage, God is always with me."

"Then we shall leave you," Giovanni said, rising. "Even those two must pay attention to a man of God."

"You must pray for my success."

"We shall certainly do that and wait anxiously for news."

Father D'Agostino had little hope in his heart as he walked briskly through the town but what was there urged him on.

He soon reached a long stone wall surrounding a white house set among pleasant greenery and flowers. Stretching to the rear were terraced vineyards where men and women worked in a pleasant setting to the sound of music and song.

"Father, Father!" One of the men came running.

"Pasquale, good day to you."

"I am glad that you are here, Father." The man was short, fat, and out of breath. "I never was so glad to see another. You are welcome. I will get you some chilled wine."

"No, thank you, Pasquale. Why are you so excited?"

"Do you not know who is here?"

"Giovanni de Lellis, your noble cousin."

"You are blessed with visions, Father. Yes, he is here, in this house, my house."

"Where may I find him, Pasquale?"

"Where else but in the kitchen drinking with that blackguard son of his?" Pasquale lowered his voice. "He rode in this morning. The two of them have been drinking for hours. No one dares to go near them for we have heard loud voices many times."

"I shall go in."

"Be careful, Father. You know that they are quarrelsome enough but with the wine they are very bad. They have both had too much to drink."

"I shall be careful."

"I will wait outside, Father. If you need me, only call."

"And what good would that do, my son?"

Pasquale had the grace to show shame. "Not much, Father. You see I am a peaceful man but not good with words or blows. If I should cross those two they would become wild. Oh, I tell you, Father, they are a pair, a real pair. It is good that my poor, dead cousin did not live to see what a sight her husband and son have become."

The priest walked through the gate to the back of the house. Voices reached him and he paused a moment to breathe a little prayer then lifted the latch and entered. Coolness and the tangy aroma of wine embraced him.

The kitchen suddenly seemed crowded as two figures came to their feet. They were so huge of stature they dwarfed the cleric. The fine lines and delicacy of their features, their almost identical black eyes proclaimed them of close blood. The younger's hair was brown; the older's, gray. Both stared at the new arrival.

"Father!" Giovanni de Lellis cried. "This is indeed a great honor to the house of our cousin and to us."

"You are most kind in your remarks, Don Giovanni."

"May we offer you refreshment, Father?" The parent waved to the disordered table, littered with playing cards, bottles, and glasses.

"Not right now, my son." The priest turned to the young man who had remained silent. "How are you, Camillus?"

"I am well, thank you, Father."

"Is he not a fine boy, Father?" The big man poured wine into three glasses.

"Yes, Camillus is a fine figure of a boy," the priest said slowly. "I wonder what kind of a man he will be?"

"I will be a real man, do not doubt," the boy said sullenly as he accepted a glass.

Don Giovanni laughed. "Do not have any fear for Camillus. He is well able to take care of himself."

"I wonder," was the reply. "Don Giovanni, do you remember how your dear wife, God bless her memory, used to pray for Camillus?"

The big man put his glass down and stared at the priest. "Why do you bring such a thing to mind at this time, Father?"

"The townspeople still call her St. Elizabeth, she was so good," the priest said gently.

"It is true. She was a holy lady and is now a saint." Giovanni searched the eyes of the visitor. "Why do you talk of her now?"

"Would she be proud of Camillus and his temper, his love of cards and brawling, his drinking?"

"This priest is forever talking like that," Camillus said angrily.

His father stood straight and tall, and spoke slowly. "This is an affront to me and mine. Were you anyone but a priest I should demand satisfaction."

"It is my duty to speak the truth, Don Giovanni. You, as the father of Camillus, must address yourself to him. No one in town dares to speak, so fierce is his temper. He has become a public scandal."

"I have had enough of this." With one mad thrust Don Giovanni sent the litter on the table crashing to the floor.

"So, too, have I," Camillus shouted equally as loud. "I have kept away from this man because of his prattling."

"You have been long absent from the sacraments, my son."

"And so I will stay." Camillus literally screamed, his face red with fury.

"Quiet, quiet!" the father ordered and the boy sullenly subsided.

"I have only this to say to you, Father," Don Giovanni said coldly. "The people of this town are not the ones to judge my son. His ways have been those of other young men. These townspeople are peasants, they live and die on a plot of land with no idea of the world. It is to them you may preach but not to my son. He is not of them."

"All belong to God."

"Have it your way but I also will have mine. I am sick

of returning to this town to hear wild outbursts against the spirit of youth. Do you know what I am going to do?" He advanced toward the priest who maintained his calmness although his heart beat faster.

"I hope that you will speak to Camillus."

The soldier had difficulty controlling his voice. "I am taking my son with me tonight. He will never again bother this town. I will rear him as a lion rears its young. Now go, go before I lose my temper and forget that you are a man of the Church."

The priest did not hurry as he came to his feet. "I will go, my friends, but I will pray constantly for you. I will think of you daily at Mass."

"Well, you may be sure that we will not think of you," Don Giovanni said with bitter sarcasm.

CHAPTER II

They came riding down the long, dusty road that stretched like a brown snake in the sun. On either side bare farm fields burned in that summer's extraordinary heat. There was no shade.

The older man rode straight; the younger slouched, the clanking armor tied to their saddles keeping time with the steady hoof beats.

Camillus marveled at the fortitude of his parent. Mile after mile his admiration increased as no sign of weariness touched Don Giovanni. "How I should like to have his strength, his courage," he told himself. Such a thought gave him the necessary reserve to hold his own painful place in the saddle.

For a long time he had restrained his tongue, subduing the almost intolerable thirst that tortured his throat, beating down the impulse that asked his aching body to stop and wait. "How I should like a cool flagon of wine," he thought.

His imagination conjured up visions of long, dark tap-rooms, the coldness of a blessed drink, the touch of a comforting breeze. Everything that mocked his heat stricken frame appeared and the only remedy Camillus used was to look at Giovanni, apparently undisturbed. "I shall never ask him to stop. He shall find no weakness in me."

The voice of his father set him erect in the saddle. "We will be there shortly, my boy."

"Where is there, Father?"

His parent turned with a smile that held a touch of teasing yet more of pride. "Do not tell me that you would not welcome a refreshing drink, a little rest, perhaps the chance to wash this country dust from your nostrils?"

"If you wish, Father."

"If I wish? Of course, if you are not of such a mind, Camillus, we could ride along. I know a fine spot a dozen miles up this very road."

"A dozen miles!"

Don Giovanni laughed. "Ah, well, we will stop beyond the bend. You have done well, Camillus. Not a single complaint. I tell you I know that you will make a real campaigner. You will be a great soldier."

Camillus was vastly pleased and at the moment would have gladly ridden the proposed dozen miles in order to impress his father.

"Now listen to me, Son." Don Giovanni's bantering tone was gone. "When we arrive at this inn you mind your place and let me do the talking. Do you understand?"

"Of course, Father." The past week had been the answer to Camillus' most longed for dreams. He was resolved not to lose them and would follow his father's injunction to the letter.

The two horses turned the bend and came into a valley where the grass was green and a silvery brook ran swiftly behind a dozen scattered, well-kept houses. The tantalizing fragrance of ripening fruit floated toward them from the heavily laden branches of an orchard and sprawling vineyards.

"We are here, my boy!" Don Giovanni easily, with no trace of fatigue, dismounted before the largest building.

Camillus climbed down more slowly, still trying to conceal the aches. He felt his legs tremble as they touched the solid earth.

His father eyed him carefully. "You have acted a fine part, Son. You do not appear the least bit tired."

"Nor am I, Father."

"Then you are a much better man than I have ever met." Don Giovanni laughed and Camillus joined him. "I myself, confidentially, am ready to pass out."

A white aproned man hurried from the largest of the buildings. "Good day, noble sirs." He waved his hands in greeting. "You are more welcome to my house than the rain is to the grass. Of course you would not deign to stay overnight in such a poor place but I shall serve you good wine and then you may pass on. It is a great honor to me, noble sirs."

"What kind of talk is this?" Don Giovanni asked sternly. "You had better give good service for we most surely intend to stay the night."

The man glanced furtively over his shoulder and lowered his voice. "There is no room. A band of evil looking soldiers have taken all the rooms. However, I shall serve you a cold flagon in the vineyard, back of the inn, a most pleasant place, yes, a most pleasant place." He smiled. "I will have your horses taken care of so that you may ride on in confidence."

A scowl settled over the face of the older De Lellis as he addressed his son. "This scoundrel is trying to drive us away. Innkeeper, do you know who I am?"

"Only that you are apparently a great lord." The man was now frightened. "I do not mean any harm."

"Then watch this." Don Giovanni strode firmly toward the door with one hand on his pommeled sword.

Camillus felt a sudden wave of exultation. "Out of my way!" he cried, pushing the proprietor from his path and ranging alongside his father as they entered the room.

Shutters had been thrown wide, unusual in the heat of the day, so their vision was excellent. A group of men, some sitting and some standing, were startled as Giovanni strode forward. "Who dares tell Giovanni de Lellis and his son there is no room for a night's rest?" he shouted.

"The devil himself!" one man cried. "It is you, Juan, and no apparition."

"Don Juan de Lellis," another echoed. "We thought you had gone over to the Turks."

"Welcome, Juan." A chorus of wild cries filled the room as the men crowded about.

Camillus, expecting trouble and relishing it, felt himself pushed back onto a bench and a cold glass of wine thrust into his hand.

"So this is the heir we have heard so much about."

"He is a replica of you, Don Juan. Let us hope that he is not so lucky at cards but as good with a blade."

"Camillus, an excellent name for a soldier."

Camillus now found that most of the assemblage called his father by the Spanish name to the complete exclusion of his native one. From now on he heard his father addressed only as Don Juan.

The innkeeper, his terror banished, wreathed his face in smiles. Some of the soldiers were clean shaven but for the most part they wore beards of various styles and looked like desperate individuals. Their attitude toward Don Juan was one of mingled respect and warm friendship.

"We are in luck, indeed, Camillus," his father said as he put down an empty glass. "These are really our friends."

"If your son is at all like you he is welcome as a friend," an especially short man said with a grin. "We have missed you, Juan, because we have had no action. When you are around, things pick up."

"No action?" De Lellis asked. "What is all this talk about the Duke fighting the Turks? I am looking to enlist and have brought my son for the same purpose."

"Oh, we will fight the Turks and we have need of every good blade."

Don Juan filled his glass. "The Turks have been a nightmare to Europe for centuries. One of us is equal to a hundred of them."

"High odds, Juan, high odds."

"Do you doubt me?"

"With no offense I question the odds. You forget they are fanatics about their religion, and every war with the hated infidel is a holy one."

"Their religious fervor does not bother me," De Lellis said. "I have had my hour with the Turks. They yield to a steel blade as readily as another."

"It is said they intend a great assault on the continent."

"So let them. It will mean more work for all of us and work that will be well paid."

The innkeeper and his two assistants appeared bearing trays of appetizing meats and vegetables steaming with mouth watering aromas. Camillus, to his overflowing pride, found himself received as an equal by these battle scarred veterans. He was beyond happiness.

"Are you waiting here for the Duke?" Don Juan glanced up from his food.

"No, we are moving in the morning. The Duke is some twenty-five miles to the north enlisting recruits."

"Excellent, excellent. We shall all ride together."

The more wine that was brought in, and it seemed to flow constantly, the more boisterous the company grew.

"How about a bout at cards?" Don Juan asked after an interval of some hours of talking and drinking.

"You are too lucky," the little man, who seemed most friendly to De Lellis, replied. "It is very seldom that you walk away the loser."

Don Juan roared. "It is Rinaldo Palleschi who talks. I recall you talked and talked and took most of my money the last time we played."

"You have a good imagination, Don Juan."

"Oh, so you do not remember? Ah, I see that you do. It is all the same to me. If you do not care to play, if you are afraid of the reputation you yourself have given me, then let us look somewhere else for an opponent."

"You have a devious tongue." The little man smiled. "You know that I have always been foolish enough to play with you. Yes, I did trim you well once but how many times have you been loaded with my money?"

"That is in the past, Rinaldo. Let us do away with all this talk. Your luck has perchance changed and you will once more outwit me." De Lellis waved his hand to the innkeeper. "Remove all this and bring new cards."

In the years to come, Camillus was to watch or participate in many games with high stakes but never was he to reach the apex of excitement that that night's play in the mountain inn gave him. Long years after, he was to recall the tense, strained faces of the players. Their hawklike eagerness never changed during the afternoon and remained the same as the hyacinth shadows deepened to the purple dark of night.

Candles were brought and the only sounds were the curt words of the players, the clink of coins, and the tinkle of bottle and glass.

Physical fatigue and mental tenseness finally caused some relaxation and after an especially close hand they would stop to exchange jests and drinks.

Camillus felt deep excitement grip him as the contest moved back and forth, the pile of coins changing size before the hunched form of his soldier father. Instinctively, he felt victory, knew that his parent must win. It was not conceivable that he could lose and his faith was increased as two of the players dropped out of the game.

Only the little man with the quiet smile was left and he was every bit as contained as Giovanni de Lellis but the coins grew fewer and fewer in his pile.

Hour after hour went by and Camillus was forced to call himself back from sleep by great exertion. Once he must have dozed for he was suddenly roused wide awake by a resounding blow upon the table and now his father and the little man were laughing.

"By the heavens, Juan, you deserve to win. You have completely wiped me out and the score is even."

Camillus looked at the large pile of glinting gold and silver in front of Don Juan. The wavering candlelight cast strange shafts of fire upon the metal. Giovanni de Lellis separated a portion and slid it across to his opponent. "You will have need of this," he said. "Do not refuse for you were good to me in Spain when the heavens smiled upon you."

"I am grateful, Don Juan." The other put the coins in his pouch.

"It has been a pleasant evening. The only thing left is bed." Don Juan tossed some coins to the table and the innkeeper hastily gathered them.

"Your room is ready, my lord. I have an excellent one, large with two separate beds. It is most comfortable. I can guarantee sound sleep."

"Then you have a unique place in the world. Lead on. We shall sleep plenty of times on the ground, Camillus. When the opportunity comes, enjoy a bed. We shall see you in the morning, my friends."

Only a few of the group remained and as Camillus followed his father he saw five of them about the table, apparently with no intention of retiring.

Their accommodations had not been exaggerated and Don Juan, smiling at his son, nodded with satisfaction as the door closed. "What have you to say now, my boy?"

"It was magnificent, Father. I have never seen anything like it. You played for hours and always remained as alert as when you had started."

"Appearances are deceitful." Giovanni laughed. "However, you have seen nothing as yet. I have played in games that lasted for weeks, time out only for sleep and hurried food as the game went on. This, of course, was in camp or at a siege when there was nothing else to do."

"I should love that."

"We shall see. We shall see." He reached into his wallet and produced a handful of gold, forcing it upon Camillus.

"It is more than I have ever had, Father. It is too much."

"You will have much more, my boy. You must have faith in yourself, keep calm in the face of what may appear impossible odds. Oh, you will do. I have no fear for you." A shadow passed over the older man's face. "I have made many mistakes and I shall try and see that you benefit from them."

"I shall do my best, Father, to follow your orders."

Giovanni sat on the edge of the bed. "Let us rather say my advice, not orders, son. I shall teach you to use your weapons, your tongue, and your ability so that you may reach heights I could not have you fail to know. Had I known what I do now I, too, might have reached them."

"I do not understand."

"Of course you do not. Youth cannot understand age. You will learn. You saw me at cards tonight. That is part of a soldier's life. I shall teach you details of the games, the tricks you must watch. There are many of which you have no idea."

"I shall try to please you, Father."

"I am certain that you will. You must become a great

soldier. That must be your objective. Now let us get some sleep. Tomorrow will be another day and we shall meet it as we meet all days, as a challenge to be taken up and contested."

Camillus did not sleep well that night. Despite his physical fatigue the events of the day re-enacted themselves and he tossed far into the early hours of the morning. His mind was determined. He would make his name resound on the battlefields of the world. He pondered the dreams of youth, the high vaulted ambitions, and convinced himself that the glory of the conqueror awaited him.

He watched the shaft of cold moonlight creep into the casement and cast itself across the walls and stone floor. Slowly it fingered along the room and finally came to rest upon the pallid figure of a crucified man whose bowed head looked down upon him.

Camillus stared at the statue and strange emotions coursed through him. Startled, he found himself murmuring a prayer, then fell asleep with his eyes still upon the white figure against the black crossed trees.

CHAPTER III

The year 1568 faded into oblivion and left no outstanding significance to stir a later generation. The annals of that time record no great event, yet it was the glorious start of a golden odyssey for Camillus de Lellis.

From the peaceful quiet of Bucchianico to the noisy camps of mercenaries scattered across southern Europe was the route of the gangling boy who had broadened into a swaggering bravo. His father's band was for sale to the highest bidder, and dukes and princes of Italy used them often. At one time His Holiness the Pope had needed them for policing and now they found themselves across the Adriatic Sea in the land of Mohammed. This employment by the enemy of Christendom had shocked Camillus until the explanation was made that they had not signed to battle but merely as temporary bodyguards to Ali Pasha, closest to the throne of the Sultan. Intrigue and murder had led to the importation of foreigners for protection. The sons of the Prophet feared their own followers and the all too prevalent custom of assassination.

The richness of robed splendor and the glint of varihued jewels contrasted with the dark, angry faces of the two men sitting in the sprawling tent of the Pasha.

"I tell you this, Selim." The tall man stroked his beard. "It was an evil day when they came to our camp."

His companion was short and fat, with a green sash across his white robe. He merely grunted.

"Why do you sound so much like a pig, Selim? Does the

truth hurt you? Those dogs of Christians are a villainous lot and our own men do mutter."

Selim scowled. His eyes were like slits in the fat folds of his face. "Must I tell you a hundred, yes, a thousand times, it was not my doing? I did not bring them here, Hassan. I hate them worse than wine."

The tall man walked about. "Wine, wine, where do they get it? They drink it in amazing quantities yet none is to be found in the camp. They have evil magic to conjure up this drink of the devil. They fight each other, they curse and gamble. They boast that they are not followers of the Prophet."

"It is a wicked outfit with a wicked leader. The whelp of the lion leads the pack, the son by name of Camillus."

"You must speak to the Pasha and get rid of them else their safe conduct will be forfeit," the tall man said. "I am the leader of the troops but I cannot hold back their hatred much longer. You are the confidant of the Pasha. It is you who must repeat these words."

"I have," Selim said bitterly. "I have been forbidden to mention the subject again. Must I insist upon talking to the Pasha against his will and lose my head? By the beard of the Prophet I will not do this. They were hired to protect him. If I suggest they be sent away he will think I wish to have him murdered."

"Then their blood will flow, for man cannot endure insults forever."

The other shrugged.

"They will turn on us, I tell you. Do you know how many of them wear crosses?"

The tent flap was suddenly thrown aside and a small, thin man came in, his very bearing proclaiming leadership. The two men made hasty obeisance and welcomed him loudly.

"Allah be praised for your safe return, oh, Pasha," Selim cried and his companion echoed the words.

The newcomer surveyed them with open coldness. "Why is there such muttering and murmuring in this camp? I have ears that you do not know about. Speak to me or it may be that you will not be able to speak."

"You have asked, oh worthy Pasha," the leader of the men quickly said. "Your followers, all true believers, have been subjected to insults and on some occasions even assault by the Christian dogs within our camp."

The Pasha nodded. "That is the frankness that I long for. They have served well as my bodyguard but I now have the personal palace guard of the Sultan assigned to me. I do not need the Christians."

"We are happy to know that His Highness, our beloved Sultan, is protecting the most loyal of his men. The Christians are a drunken, blasphemous lot."

The Pasha fingered a purse then flung it to the table. "Go at once and bring the Christian leader, Don Juan De Lellis, to me."

"Say but the word and we will fall upon the debauched lot."

"No, I have given my word for their safe conduct."

Within the space of a few minutes the tall Moslem returned accompanied by Don Juan. The Mohammedan leader carefully regarded the soldier. He liked this Christian and regretted he could not have him on his side permanently.

"I was on my way to see you, noble Pasha," Don Juan said pleasantly. "It was a pleasure to meet your messenger bearing word that you desired to talk."

"What pleasure there is shall be seen." The Pasha picked up the moneybag. "Here is the pay I promised you for next month."

"It is not necessary to pay us in advance."

"You are going on a journey," the Pasha said. "I trust it will be a pleasant one for you and your men. You are to return to Italy for you are no more in my service."

"You are dissatisfied with us?"

"Our ways are as the ways of the sun and the moon. We will never meet. You and your soldiers must be out of this camp within the hour."

"Within the hour? It is scant time, oh Pasha. May I ask the reason why?"

"You may." The Moslem smiled. "There have been many complaints of drinking, gambling, and fighting. I do not intend to tolerate the behavior of your men."

"I am sure the reports are greatly exaggerated."

"If anything they have been understated. I shall not change my mind."

"If this be so, let it be." Don Juan accepted the pouch. "Thank you for your generosity. Perhaps we shall meet again under more pleasant circumstances."

"I doubt that the circumstances will be more pleasant," the Pasha replied with his ready smile. "It is not because of you that I have given my orders. It is your men. You will leave within the hour and safe conduct to the coast and waiting boats will be yours."

Don Juan's temper was not the best as he went into the section of the camp reserved for his group. The sight that met his eyes only infuriated him. Some of the Christians were reclining at ease but the majority were in a huddle over a dice game.

"Get up, you fools," the leader cried. "We are ordered to leave this place within the hour. We have been discharged by the Pasha."

Camillus came forward. "What is this you are saying?"

"It is those infernal dice. Everywhere that you gather it is to throw dice or play at cards. The Pasha has sickened of your actions and has ordered us from the camp giving us but an hour's grace."

"Since when have you hated gambling, Juan?" someone called.

"I, at least, have known my place here." The leader's voice sharpened. "Where else will you get such pay? The Pasha has not seen me tossing a handful of coin on the turn of a card. If I have played it has been behind the walls of a tent. There is no time for argument. Get your gear and saddle the horses. Our safe conduct is but for one hour and we must proceed to the coast at once."

"The infidel dog!"

"Let us give them a taste of our swords before we leave."

"You are all fools," Don Juan said bitterly. "We are a mere handful against thousands. They would carve us to bits."

It was a silent, disgruntled lot that wound its way through the tented streets of the Turkish encampment. Silence greeted them everywhere, a silence augmented by the hatred in thousands of eyes.

Camillus, riding at his father's side, finally broke the heavy silence. "There are other armies, Father. I am sorry if I have contributed to this affair."

"There are other armies but with no such pay as this one provided. You do not know our friends who ride with us. This is the end of our band. When the Italian coast is reached you will see them leave."

"Oh, I do not think so."

"I know so. They are only with us because they were promised much money and an easy time in the service of the Turk. Service is difficult to obtain when it must be taken in groups. Individually, they will all do well."

"The men cannot blame you."

"I fear not their blame nor do I welcome their praise. It is only that they will now seek separate fortunes. The band is broken. You and I will find ourselves quite alone when we have arrived on the mainland."

Camillus, on friendly terms with the men and knowing their admiration for his father, was inclined to disagree, but in this he was wrong. Two weeks later he sat opposite Don Juan in the inn of a remote town in northern Italy.

"You see," his father said. "I knew the men. Now, my son, what do you propose?"

"We have gold, Father, and we can rest for a while without making a hasty decision. I am glad that we severed all of our connections with the Turks. I did not relish fighting alongside the infidel, although my sword, thank God, was never raised against a Christian in the interests of another religion."

"I knew from the beginning that you were adverse to the alliance. I am happy that you, at least, followed your father."

"Let us forget the whole matter and take a good rest."

"Well," Don Juan hesitated, then spoke uneasily. "We cannot afford to rest too long a time."

"Cannot afford to rest too long a time? You forget that we have two shares of the Pasha's gold!"

Don Juan flushed and it was with difficulty that he spoke. "We had two shares," he said. "While you were winning, Camillus, I was losing."

"So that is it." Camillus cleared his throat and tried to keep disappointment from his voice. "Well, so be it. What shall we now do?"

"Work," Don Juan said humbly. "And the only work we know is the sword."

"Have you anyone in mind?"

"There is a great expedition being fitted out," was the slow reply. "Venice and Spain and the Pope along with a great many princes are building ships and hiring soldiers. It is said that the great Admiral Doria is to head an expedition against the Turks."

"I should like that," the son said affectionately, feeling sorry at his father's humiliation. "At least we will be together."

"We shall receive a ready welcome in Venice."

"What if they have heard of our recent association with the Turks?"

"Likely they will," Don Juan said calmly. "Tongues will talk and ears will listen. It will not hurt us. They know that our swords are good. Perhaps I can sell the Duke of Venice some information about the infidel."

"I am anxious for this adventure."

"Let us drink to our new enterprise. We shall rest the night and tomorrow be on our way."

Camillus stood up, a sudden touch of agony upon his face.

"What is it?" Don Juan was deeply concerned.

"It is my leg again, Father."

"We must see some good doctor in Venice. They have many there. You have had trouble with that leg for some time."

"For the past few months."

"That is too long. Let me look at it. No, sit down."

Don Juan busied himself with the inspection. "The skin is broken. I do not like the looks of it." He called the innkeeper to bring a doctor as soon as possible. "We shall be more at ease if someone with knowledge looks at it." He poured two glasses of wine.

The innkeeper returned in a short time with a thin, quiet young man. "This is my cousin, noble sirs. We are very fortunate to have him with us for a short stay. He is returning to Rome to further his studies and is only here to visit. I am sure he will be able to help."

"Were you wounded?" the medical man asked after a brief inspection.

"I cannot account for it. Every so often my foot and ankle become inflamed. The itch is unbearable."

"The skin is broken, perhaps from scratching. You also have symptoms on the instep and lower leg."

"What is it?" Don Juan asked impatiently.

"It is not a disease known to me. I have a salve that will give you relief but it will only be temporary. This is a strange sore, a sort of ulcer."

"It drives me frantic from itching." Camillus winced at the probing. The doctor continued his medication and Camillus was glad when the cooling salve finally stopped the irritation.

"I advise you to get further treatment," the doctor said as he stood up to go. "It is a deep-seated sore. If you could go to some city hospital and stay there for constant treatment you might get results. Moving about the country with inadequate care will only aggravate it."

"From what I have seen and heard about hospitals I should never want a son of mine in one of them," said Don Juan. "They are charnel houses, built only to receive the living dead."

"It is true that some are hospitals in name only," the other said. "Well, that is my advice. You must have continuous care. I still say a hospital could provide it."

"I would have none of them," said Don Juan.

"Nor would I," said Camillus.

CHAPTER IV

The highway to the north was an ancient one, built in the dim, distant past by slave labor under the whip of the Caesars. It wound through the low marshlands, steaming in the summer heat, up past the cool greenery of farmlands, climbing, climbing, until at last it disappeared beneath the white cloak of mountain snow.

If the worn stones could cry out they would tell hitherto untold tales of conquerors and conquered, Christian and pagan invaders, of villains and saints. It could even speak of unknown priests journeying to Rome to become vicars of Christ on earth, plucked from the hidden recesses of God's vineyard to occupy the mightiest of thrones.

The road lay waiting for new stories to hide beneath its hard surface as in the bitter heat of the mid-months of 1569 two horsemen moved slowly forward, two whose names were to be legend to millions yet unborn, one because of what he did, and one because he was the father of this man who was to write his name indelibly across the pages of time.

It was on this road that God spoke for the first time to Camillus de Lellis and His voice was in the sharp sword of sorrow. He had conquered Paul on the road to Tarsus and He was to conquer Camillus de Lellis on the road to Ancona, not immediately, but by moving the first pawn in the game of chess that was to decide between sinner and saint.

For over a year Camillus and his father had worked in the service of Venice and were now on their way north after a short vacation in the southlands, a vacation of riotous and quarrelsome occupation.

"This is a new route for me, Father," the son said. "When do we stop for a rest? You seem anxious to move along as if you had some appointment."

"We can reach Ancona, Camillus. There is a garrison there where we may stop and have good company. Do not fret. It is not too far distant."

"I sometimes wonder if we should seek service other than with the Duke of Venice. He seems to be waiting for everyone to move before he takes any definite steps."

Don Juan laughed. "That is the impatience of youth. Time will take care of all. Let us not hurry, my boy."

"Well, it is tiresome."

"Of course it is. Remember, each minute we live is one less for us to enjoy. You will see plenty of action in your time. At last the Old Man in Rome has opened his money pouch and many galleons are being built. Prince John of Austria is to lead a great expedition against the stronghold of the Turk. You will have your long desired wish to fight for Christendom."

Camillus was silent. Violent, quarrelsome, addicted to all games of chance, he always felt annoyance at his father's light reference to religion. He, himself, occasionally prayed.

He studied the strange man beside him. Years of fast living and violent action seemed to have made no marked change in the handsome face and figure. Lean, spare, and strong, he was far more enduring than men thirty years his junior. The hair was iron gray but the face hardly lined, handsome and tanned beneath the suns of a dozen countries.

What concerned Camillus was his father's inconsistency in the matter of religion. Though he might hire his sword to the infidel for gold and treat ecclesiastical matters lightly, never had he failed to bless himself or to take time at wayside shrines. His moral code was a rigid one and he never frequented questionable houses or companions.

Camillus, too, had a deep contempt for the vices that beset his companions, other than drinking, gambling, and fighting. These latter he indulged in but the more deadly sin he looked upon with disgust as a definite sign of weakness.

Don Juan was in a rare talkative mood. He now paid a most cherished compliment to Camillus and revealed the true side of his own character. "You are not only a soldier but a man fit to face his own mother, here or in heaven," he said, looking sharply at his son. "You know, Camillus, that is the real test of a man, that he does not lose himself in the vices of the weak."

They rode in silence until the father again broke into conversation. "I can still face Camilla de Compellis," he said, mentioning the maiden name of the boy's mother. "I do not owe her an apology for any of my actions. I have been true to her." This pattern of morality, set by the father, was to govern the son during the wildest days of his expeditions.

Camillus wanted his father to keep on talking. "Isn't it strange, Father," he asked, "that I was born so late in life?"

Don Juan shrugged. "Some call it a miracle and well it may have been. Your mother was a very fine lady. All the townspeople called her St. Elizabeth because she was three score years old when you were born. She had prayed constantly for you. She had a dream, a constant dream, that she saw you with a red cross on your breast carrying a standard with many following you."

"I recall her talking of such a dream."

"It may be that you will be a great soldier. I have taught you all I know. Remember this, though, there is no greatness without opportunity. Whomsoever you serve, serve well. You may rise to a high position so that future generations will point to you with admiration and say, 'There was a real soldier.'"

This was the ambition of Camillus and his father's words only served to renew it.

"I do not like sermons, Camillus. I feel, however, that I should speak to you. I love and have loved gambling all my days. It is in your very blood. I must tell you, nevertheless, I might have risen much higher in life if I had ignored the gambling urge. If you would put it in its proper place you might benefit accordingly."

Camillus laughed. "Come now, Father," he said. "You know that I am very capable."

"That is true. So, too, am I. What has it gained me? One must learn for himself. Look," he pointed down the road. "There is the village of Loretto and it is there we shall stop and push on to the garrison tomorrow. The fort of San Lupido is outside the town but I should like to have this night with you. It is a good inn so let us make haste."

Even after an excellent meal and a sampling of good wine a feeling of uneasiness pervaded Camillus. He felt a strange disturbance at his father's habit of retrospection that had been showing itself during the past few days. It almost seemed as if Don Juan was attempting to turn his son into channels other than those he had traveled his own lifetime.

"You must remember," Don Juan said in the course of conversation, "your services will be watched in this coming campaign. It may well mark the turning point of your career. The Duke of Venice is well acquainted with our name and he has already marked you. This I know. I have high hopes for you, my son."

"I shall try to live up to them by being a real soldier. Never fear our name will be sullied by a dishonorable act."

"That I know." Don Juan paused to pass his hand over his face. "Lately, I have had a strange feeling that I cannot definitely explain."

"What do you mean by that, Father?"

"It is a strange sensation, as I have said, but at times it is accompanied by slight pains in my arms and chest. Tonight, in fact just now, I have felt them returning. I expect it is a cold and nothing more."

"Is there anything I can do?"

"No, it will pass."

Camillus studied his father's face. "You do not look your usual self, Father."

"Yes, yes, I know." Don Juan impatiently waved his hand. "It is only that I have hardly ever been ill, even in the midst of plague. I think I must finally be getting old." He forced a laugh. "Perhaps I should retire to bed."

"An excellent idea."

Camillus went to the door leading to the kitchen and called the innkeeper. "My father is to be shown to his room at once."

"It is ready." The man advanced toward the sitting soldier then turned with an expression of alarm. "He does not look well. He is very pale and shaking."

It was true. The color had fled from the face of the old soldier, paler now beneath his tan, and a fit of trembling shook his body. He tried but could not get to his feet. He waved their proffered help to one side and finally, exerting a great effort, managed to stand. Then he staggered and, except for Camillus, would have fallen.

"Perhaps it is the sun," the innkeeper suggested. "Then again it may have been the wine."

"You idiot," Camillus said, thoroughly alarmed. "We have been out of the sun for hours and we have not even begun to drink. My father is ill. Send for a doctor at once."

"No, no, Camillus. I will be all right in a few minutes."

Camillus openly defied his parent for the first time in his life. "Get the physician," he said sternly to the proprietor. "Give me help to get him to his room. He is really ill. Hurry."

Don Juan, almost helpless, was led down the stone corridor and with much protestation placed in his bed.

"Where is the doctor?" Camillus cried, grasping the innkeeper by the tunic.

"He has been sent for, Excellency. Did you not see my son running from the taproom?" The man was frightened. As if to echo the statement the doctor arrived and immediately went to work.

Camillus stood in a corner of the chamber and watched with a helpless feeling, noting the laborious heaving of his father's chest and the perspiration running down his face.

"He is unconscious," the physician said.

"What is the matter with him?"

"He has lived long and fast but he has tremendous reserves of strength. A fit of the ague has touched him and his heart is not responding too well."

"I want him to live," Camillus cried. "Tell us that there is no danger."

"I cannot lie to you. I, too, want him to live but he will be dead by morning."

"Dead? That cannot be. No, no, that cannot be."

"It is the truth and I am sorry to tell you. You should send for a priest. I am useless here. Only a priest can help him now."

"A priest?"

"Most certainly. He alone can save him, but not for this life. I am sorry."

Camillus was stunned by the sudden turn of events and his world, created around Don Juan, whirled madly.

"Shall I send for the priest?" the innkeeper asked.

"Yes, of course. Get him at once. Maybe the holy sacraments will help him."

Camillus did not move from the doorway but continued to stare at the once powerful figure helpless on the bed. He did not remember the arrival of the priest but he awakened from his trance to hear the intoned Latin words. "I cannot realize that he will die," he muttered.

Don Juan rallied in the early hours of the morning and regained consciousness. The priest waved Camillus from the room while he heard the confession of the old soldier and then brought the youth back to the bedside.

Don Juan, his eyes bright with fever, recognized his son. "Ah, it is good to have you with me," he whispered. "Stay, do not go."

"Have no fear that I will leave, Father."

There was a long pause and finally Don Juan spoke in a clearer voice. "It is the end of the road. You have pleased me greatly. I thank you for calling the priest. After all, he is the most important one at an affair like this." He managed to smile. "At last I can face your mother. You know, she used to worry that I might die without the sacraments. Well, I have had them."

Some time later he spoke again. "Do not forget what I have told you. Serve your leader well. I shall wait for you and if it is possible I shall watch over you. You will be a great soldier. Of this I do not doubt."

Camillus did not answer. Gently he kept hold of his father's hand.

The dawn cast its first gray fingers into the room when Camillus felt a limpness in the fingers of Don Juan. His father was dead. He threw himself to his knees and cried out to heaven, weeping openly.

The comforting hand of the priest was on his shoulder. "It is but the beginning for him, my son. You must not weep."

But Camillus de Lellis wept on.

CHAPTER V

The day following the burial Camillus came down with fever and for three days battled to live. His strong constitution asserted itself and, although he recovered from the fever, the ailment affecting his right ankle and foot grew worse. The village priest proved to be an excellent friend and it was his concern that carried Camillus through those dark days.

Camillus now had no place to turn. His funds were low and the sore on his leg caused much difficulty even in walking. More than once, in his distressed mind, he dreamed of seeking refuge in some monastery but almost immediately abandoned the idea, so unworthy did he believe himself.

Bucchianico came into his mind but Camillus felt his proud spirit rebel. The people would whisper and laugh in private at the returned soldier and this he could not bear. "I shall go and serve with the Duke of Venice," he resolved, but the thought was not so pleasant without the company of Don Juan.

One day the priest found him standing in the garden, gazing off at the horizon. "It is a beautiful day, my son. I am glad to see that you are returning to your old self."

Camillus was about to make a bitter reply but the kindly tones stopped him. "He is not an easy man to forget, Father."

"No. Parents are never easy to forget. Your father was an extraordinary man and your constant companion. He is better off, this you must believe."

"If I did not believe that, Father, regardless of how I have lived, there would be nothing left for me."

"Your leg wound still bothers you. I have seen you walking and it must be painful."

"It is not a wound, Father. Certainly I would remember a wound."

"Well, wound or not, it should have regular treament. Sometimes these little matters, if neglected, become dangerous."

"When I am in Venice I shall see the best of doctors."

"If you would let me help I think I could give you some temporary relief. There are simple remedies of the peasant that often do excellent work."

"I am ready and grateful to try anything."

"Then if you are of such a mind, let us go to my home."

Camillus experienced comfort in the curate's company. He was glad to walk with him along the dusty street, aware that he cut a fine figure in his colorful costume, sword and dagger. So immense was his pride that he exerted a terrific physical demand upon his injured leg and did not limp.

Inside the cool, stone house the priest assumed command. Camillus watched while his host brought a basin of water, clean bandages, and ointment. "It is a bad infection," the cleric said, inspecting the raw sore. "I shall wash it and then see what we can do."

"No, no, Father. I cannot have you do this."

"Why not? His Holiness washes the feet of beggars following the custom set by the Lord Himself. I am honored to do this for you." The priest went steadily about his work.

Camillus leaned back, marveling at the gentle touch, relief flooding him as the salve was applied.

"You must take better care of this or you will have much trouble," the priest said. When the work was completed he took away the utensils and returned with wine.

Camillus sipped the drink. "Father, you are not only an excellent doctor, but also a fine winemaker."

The cleric laughed. "I do not make the wine. Now, you must take this salve with you. I will give you clean bandages and you are to dress it daily until you get some competent treatment."

"You are most kind."

The priest looked at him with grave eyes. "I am not presuming to tell you what to do, Camillus, but I must say that if you go into service again your leg will receive scant attention. Am I right? There is little done for the sick, unless at battle time?"

"And not much even then, Father."

"If you could rest and take daily treatments you might become well."

"I cannot rest, Father."

"You may be forced to do just that."

"Do you know of any hospital that I might get into?"

"There are many but one stands out in my mind. It is a great hospital in the city of Rome. While I was there it was doing excellent work along many lines. Possibly it could help you."

"Rome. That is a good distance and I am not going in that direction."

"Well, it is up to you. Perhaps you could not gain admission to this place anyway. It is constantly overcrowded. It is the Hospital of St. Giacomo for the Incurables. Do not let the name alarm you. Many have left there in perfect health. It takes care of ailments other than those which may not be cured. It would be difficult to gain admission unless someone of prestige spoke for you."

Camillus rose to his feet and suddenly realized that he felt better than he had for many days. "I have an uncle who is a Capuchin Guardian at Acquila. Do you think he has sufficient influence to get me admitted?"

"He may have just the right amount of influence. After all, he is the head of a religious community. Yes, I would say that you should go to him and ask help. What is blood worth if not to help one of your own kin in need?"

Camillus placed a gold coin, one of the few he had left, on the table.

"I do not want money, Camillus. I did this for friendship."

"That I well know, Father. The coin is for the same thing. Perhaps it will help someone as you have helped me."

"I shall see that it does. If you must go, go with God's blessing." The curate followed the soldier to the gate and made the sign of the cross over him.

"I shall return someday, Father, and prove that I am not ungrateful."

"There is no need to prove that. I shall pray for you."

Camillus paid his bill at the inn, mounted his horse, and sadly turned from the spot where he had known so much sorrow. Alone, he again was assailed by fear and indecision. "Perhaps the priest is right. If I go to Venice I may be refused service because of this ailment."

He rode on for hours and finally came to the crossroads where he paused for a short rest. Stretching north was the road to Venice and possibly the glory he had sought so long, the same glory that had been the goal of the man laid away in the earth a few miles back. To the south a dusty trail led to the Eternal City and certain weeks of hospital treatment. Ever impetuous, he turned the animal in the direction of Rome and immediately felt a rise in spirits.

"The Father is right. The leg must be treated and made better before I take up soldiering again. But how will I live? I have little money. The coin is going fast and there is none to replace it. I must give this thought. Perhaps the treatment in Rome will not take too long."

Near Fermo he saw two friars coming along the road. He immediately dismounted and approached them. "Greetings, worthy brothers," he called. "I am Camillus de Lellis. Do you know the Guardian of the Friary of St. Bernardino at Acquila? Would he still be Father Compellis?"

"Yes, that is his name."

"He is my uncle." Camillus suddenly realized the pride in his voice might not be duplicated by his relative who up to this time had disapproved of him.

"A worthy guardian. You are honored, sir."

"Thank you. I have not seen him for some time. I thought I would stop there."

"He would be most pleased."

"Thank you." Camillus thought of the few coins he had left and then with characteristic impetuosity handed one of them to the friars. "For the poor," he said magnanimously.

"God's blessing upon you, noble sir."

As he resumed his journey doubts again assailed him. "Those men are at least happy," he told himself. "They have a well ordered plan. What did military honor ever avail my father? Perhaps my dear mother was right. There must be peace in prayer."

He toyed once more with the idea of religion and was tempted by the prospect. "I shall speak to my uncle," he vowed. "I shall go to him and he will counsel me. At least I may gain admission to this hospital of St. Giacomo. I will sell my horse and have a few pieces of gold to carry me along."

Camillus had that faculty of conceiving an idea and putting it into immediate action. He sold the horse at the next town and then began his journey on foot.

Difficulties multiplied. The leg that rested while he rode now rebelled at walking. The pain increased to a point where he felt that another mile would kill him, yet he kept on. The road was filled with ruts and rocks and progress was a sore trial. He cut a branch from a tree and put it to good use as a walking cane.

Thoughts of his uncle brought back childhood memories of his frequent visits with the priest. Camillus had always thought the cleric boring and had paid him scant attention. He hoped that this would not be remembered.

His mind was more at peace than it had been for a long time and when he finally reached the monastery was cheered by a very cordial reception. The old priest was overjoyed to see his sister's son but refused to ask questions until Camillus was given the opportunity of a hot bath, a good meal, and a night's sleep.

It was midmorning of the following day when Camillus sat down to talk with him. He found himself suggesting that he be given the chance to enter an order, preferably the same one as his uncle's.

Father Compellis was not impressed by his nephew's protestations. The long history of Don Juan and the shorter one of his son were all too well known. Now after so many years in that background, having his nephew mention such an ambition was unbelievable. "It is a great surprise, Camillus," he said, giving himself time to think.

"I can see that you believe I should fail as a Franciscan."

"Who am I to say that? Right now you are overwrought, disillusioned by your father's death and your present leg ailment. If Don Giovanni were alive, and may God have mercy on his soul, would you not still be with him?"

"I suppose so," Camillus said ungraciously.

"Then yours is not the true calling. When the Lord has called one to serve Him there is nothing else in life but that. I would encourage you to give it further thought and much prayer. If you are of the same mind within a year I shall do my best to foster your desire. In the meantime I suggest that your leg be given attention."

Camillus was disappointed but his pride forced him to conceal his chagrin. "I know that the leg demands treatment, Father. It is my understanding that it might be possible for you to ask admission for me to a hospital in Rome called St. Giacomo. Do you know the place?"

"It is very well known to me."

"Then you will be able to ask for my entrance?"

The priest did not answer at once and appeared to be in deep thought.

"Have you nothing to say, Uncle?" Camillus finally asked.

"Yes, I have much to say, Camillus. In fact I could think of no hospital better able to assist you. I will certainly do my utmost to gain your admission."

"Then why do you hesitate?" Camillus was annoyed. "I have a little money, not much, but I will pay for what I ask."

"This treatment may take longer than your money will last. I will obtain your admission and also try to locate a place for you in the employment of the hospital."

"What? Do you mean that I should work in the hospital?" Camillus was aghast.

"You do not have the money to pay for your treatment," the Guardian said simply. "It is better to work out your debt than to accept charity, or would you have it otherwise?"

"I want no charity," Camillus declared hotly.

"That is a good principle if you can afford it," the priest said. "Now, may I ask you a few questions?"

"What questions?" Camillus asked roughly. "Do I have to go through a veritable inquisition from a blood relative because I am forced to ask a favor?"

"You must listen to me or I will do nothing," the uncle replied firmly. "You forget that for years your late father and, yes, you yourself have followed the kind of life that makes these questions necessary."

"Get on with them, then."

"I must have your promise that you will abide by the rules of the hospital." The priest laid stress upon the words. "You will forego gambling and quarreling while you are there."

"Gambling, quarreling? Where am I going? Is this place a soldier's camp or a hospital?"

"You must promise."

"You need have no fear of my actions."

The uncle patiently studied the flushed face of his nephew. "You are quick tempered and it would be better to restrain yourself. However, I shall say no more. Your actions shall speak for you. I shall immediately write a letter which you will take to the director at the hospital."

"I am glad that that is settled," Camillus said sullenly.

The following day, armed with the sealed letter and his uncle's blessing, the youth set out for the Eternal City and its famous hospital.

CHAPTER VI

St. Giacomo was in such demand that it was almost impossible to find a vacant bed in the far-flung wards of the great institution. Large gardens and orchards bordering the main buildings lent an air of charm and restfulness but within the place the sick suffered the indignities of neglect and abuse.

The attempt to mitigate disease was sponsored by successive pontiffs and cardinals who devoted great sums of money but were handicapped by the universal ignorance then prevalent in the field of medicine. The fear of hospitals was so great that the authorities were forced to employ whom they could find. Poor men were put to work, and sometimes criminals and even condemned men were taken in as part expiation of their punishment.

Most of the patients were admitted only to die, often without benefit of the holy sacraments. Material comforts, in the hands of incompetents, were scarce and in many cases sold to outside sources for a meager profit, rather than distributed. Men were left without food, drink, or clean linen.

Brutal attendants, out of sight of sparse authority, maltreated the sick, tied them to beds, even beat them without compunction. Fraudulent compacts were often made between petty hospital officials and merchandise dealers. The Church, unaware of these private atrocities, continued to pour money into the work of serving the sick.

Camillus de Lellis, enrolled at the hospital, found himself completely disgusted with his situation and his colleagues.

He was one of the hired help, an attendant who helplessly watched the wretched inmates in their last grapple with life.

The first night of his employment found him in the rooms set aside for the workers, his mind disturbed almost to the point of open revolt.

"A scurrilous lot," he bitterly remarked, comparing his present company with the former hearty and generous, if somewhat dissipated, companions of sword and cloak. The pallid, unhealthy skin of the hospital corps made most of them look as if they should also be patients. Many times during the day it had required utmost exertion on his part to refrain from laying violent hands upon some of his co-workers, so cruel had been their treatment of the helpless.

"They are certainly the dregs of the city," he muttered.

"You do not appear too cheerful, friend." A burly man sat down near him.

"I see nothing here to make me cry out with joy."

"Oh, it is not such a bad place if you get the right frame of mind. The beds are good and our food is at least fit to eat."

Camillus looked steadily at the big man. "These people are treated worse than any I have ever seen."

"They are better off here than dying in the street. I hear that you were a soldier. I did not know that sympathy was part of the make-up of the military."

"Neither is unnecessary cruelty," Camillus said. "These dogs that treat the sick should be treated themselves."

"Well, I shall stay only until I have a few scuderi," the other replied. "How is it that you are here? Are there no wars?"

"I have a bad sore on my foot and ankle. I am here merely for treatment."

"You cannot get better doctors than we have. The only trouble is that they do not have sufficient time to take care of so many people. You will be looked after because you are a member of the staff."

"That is what I understand."

"Then you should be able to stand this place until you are better."

"Anybody that could like this work and endure it for any time is either a saint or a fool."

"Or hungry."

"What food I have had was not the makings of a banquet but I have seen worse."

"Well, keep up your courage. Oh, my name is Allesandro Corbini."

Camillus answered reluctantly. "I am Camillus de Lellis."

"Ah, a noble name."

"And what is that to you?" Camillus took offense immediately. "Do you wish to make something of my name?"

"Not in the least. You are not the first one of noble lineage to care for the sick. I meant no offense."

Camillus relented a little. "Tell me," he said, "where else can I get constant treatment? I simply give my services for services received."

"All hospitals are like this. You would be happier if you realized that this place is the best of all of them."

"God should have pity on the other hospitals, then. The stench of the wards is almost unbearable. It is worse than a battlefield three days old."

Corbini shrugged. "It is the lot of the sick. What else can be done?"

Camillus had the viewpoint of the disciplined soldier. "They are not even clean."

"Then you start cleaning them, my friend," Corbini said slyly. "We are few, the sick are many. They are going to die, anyway."

The duties of Camillus were hateful and he forced himself, looking forward to the brief treatment his own wound received each day, hoping that he would soon leave the place, dreaming always of the outside world. His only comfort was that the wound was healing even if the process was all too slow. Natural impatience kept him on edge and caused his companions not to cross him. He did not hesitate to use physical force and after the few usual tricks accorded a newcomer had been tried and answered with violence he was left alone.

Each night he tossed on his bed, longing for the day of his release. At times the memory of Don Juan crowded in on him and tears came to his eyes as he imagined what his father must think of his lowly station.

The stone walls, the ever present smell of the hospital, the tasteless food, the monotonous whimpering of the sick all goaded his restless soul. A sense of futility crept over him and his nervous tension increased. At different times he roundly beat two of his colleagues for foisting their work upon him. Thereafter they regarded him with respectful fear and his sullen manner did nothing to improve their relations.

The miserable lot of the sick enraged his sense of justice. He never neglected anyone but found that it was impossible to care for even his own patients adequately. "Is there nothing to help these people? They certainly are brought here only to die," he said one day to Corbini.

"I have told you before it is better to die here in a dirty bed than in the street. Be of good cheer. You will not be here long."

"It is over three months and I have counted each hour."

"What you need is relaxation. Do you play at cards?"

The question coursed through the veins of the soldier like a draught of brandy. "Cards? Of course I play cards, but they are forbidden here."

46 / ST. CAMILLUS

"Have you ever seen the authorities visit our rooms? There is usually a little game, late at night, when those not interested have retired."

"To think you have been playing cards while I was sleeping!" Camillus felt a sudden lifting of his spirits. "I shall be glad to join you."

The hospital players were no match for the skillful hands of De Lellis. After the first round of cards he knew he was the master of all the pasty, eager faces crowded around the table. Once again life had assumed a purpose and the old passion for games of chance gripped him. He almost forgot his desire to leave, so eager was he to sit with his new friends and match cards and dice. Life became better and his riches grew greater with every game.

Never before had his companions seen such luck as that which attended Camillus. Night after night his winning streak continued. The hospital became tolerable to him, the food fair, his wretched charges not too bad, and his now sullen colleagues amusing.

"You are a consistent winner," Corbini said, not with envy, for after a few games he had quit and was content to watch.

"It is the cards."

"There are some who say otherwise."

"But not to me, my friend," Camillus flared.

"No, not to you for they fear your temper. Listen, any man who wins all the time is never popular."

They were alone in the room waiting for their companions. "Which means what?" Camillus asked.

"Do not become angry with me." Corbini was a calm man. "I know these people. They are poor enough and now you have made them even more so. Have you not observed them of late?"

"I have noticed nothing different."

"Their work about the hospital, poor as it has always been, is worse. In time even the authorities will recognize this. Someone will talk and you will go."

"I do not care for informers," Camillus said angrily.

"You would not know it. I would suggest that you leave our companions alone. Come with me over to the ships that dock in the Tiber. There are always games there and I have been quite lucky the past few months. You should do even better."

Camillus nodded, for the other's remarks made sense. "I think you have spoken wisely. I certainly shall go with you on your next visit."

Camillus accordingly transferred his card playing to the waterfront where he did amazingly well. He found himself almost contented and returned to the hospital from these trips in a much higher frame of mind and in better spirits than he had enjoyed for many months. The sailors were far more congenial company. There was plenty of wine and he was once more enjoying life.

One night as he arrived back at the hospital he was confronted by the Maestro di Casa and two members of the hospital board. "You are coming in quite late, Camillus." The Maestro spoke in a quiet voice.

"I did not know that I was supposed to be back at any certain hour, sir. I am off duty call."

"We are aware of that. However, last week and the week before you left the hospital during hours that you were supposed to be working."

"There was little to be done during the late night hours." Camillus was calm but sensed trouble.

"That is no excuse. Apparently the only thing you care to do is play cards with the river boatmen."

"Ah, so you know where I have been," said Camillus. "Then away with all this bickering. Why do you question me at this hour?"

"The hospital authorities have kept their side of our bargain. You have been here almost nine months and your wound is practically cured. You have received the best of treatment. In return you have given us work that is by no means exceptional. We are used to that type of labor but now we have proof that most of your leisure time has been spent in gambling."

"What I do with my own time is my own business. If I care to go to the Tiber boats and play cards it is of no concern to anyone."

"It is what you do in the hospital during your off hours that we find interesting." The Maestro still spoke calmly. "We know that you have won most of the earnings of your fellow workers. You have broken the hospital rules by leaving during your hours of duty. In my office is a pack of cards removed from your mattress. That alone can dismiss you."

"I have no intention of lying to you or anyone else," Camillus said with much anger. "What you have said is the truth. Now what next?"

"You should know the answer. It is better that you leave us."

"You are putting me out?"

"We are asking you to leave."

Camillus flamed. "I shall go and gladly. My stomach is certainly not for this work. Hospitals are nothing but death traps and this one is no exception. You will never see me again. I would rather die in the street than in a charnel house such as this."

"You may stay until the morning. The hour is late."

"You are most kind," Camillus said scornfully. "I do not

need your indulgence. I shall leave within the hour and if necessary sleep in the street. It will be better than here."

"Let it be as you wish. May God go with you."

"He certainly is not here." Camillus turned away with a sneer.

CHAPTER VII

The decks of the powerful galley REAL, flagship of Don Juan of Austria, commander of the magnificent fleet, were crowded to the rails with the choice troops of Spain and Italy. Only sufficient room was allowed the sailors to perform their duties. Areas around the formidable guns were marked off and no one but the gunners permitted in the restricted sections. The rest of the huge ship was given over to the hardy troops who stood ready to board and battle the enemy in personal combat.

Only those of tried courage and proved worth had been selected by Don Juan for the flagship. These men had been tested on many battlefields and were calm and confident, unmindful that each sweep of the long oars, each puff on the flaring sails, brought them closer to the Turk.

Don Pedro de Sepolevede, captain in charge of the bow, had carefully selected fifty of the best combat troops and had placed them in strategic positions. It was apparent that they would be the first to meet the foe and among them was Camillus de Lellis. These men, hard bitten by experience, showed little concern but spent their time, from excellent points of vantage, examining the greatest fleet ever gathered by Christendom, stretching over three miles in all directions.

To the left was the Venetian leader, Barbarigo, with sixty-four galleys. To the right was Marcantonio Colonna, chief of the papal forces, and Requeanes, the Spanish leader, with an array of boats that seemed to reach endlessly across the

Mediterranean. The most famous admiral of the day, Gian Andrea Doria of Genoa, at the head of approximately one hundred vessels, covered the more exposed wing of the armada. Under the command of the Marquis of Santa Cruz a reserve force of fifty galleys was directly behind the center with orders to attack in case of a Turkish breakthrough. Two hundred and eight craft, fifty thousand trained naval men, and thirty-one thousand experienced mercenaries made up the great assemblage.

Flags of every color and shape, the standards of countries, cities, towns, and noble houses, fluttered from the ropes and spars while from the masthead floated the Image of Christ against a background of all conceivable hues. Flashing lances, swords, and gleaming breastplates blinded the eyes when chance rays of a hiding sun filtered through for brief moments.

Captain de Sepolevede walked the bow section, his keen eyes accounting for all of his men. "Be of good cheer, boys. We shall have action before nightfall."

"Well, I certainly hope so." Camillus looked up from cleaning his immaculate weapons. "We can then sleep for the night instead of watching. I have heard that the Turk has fled," Camillus said, half in jest.

"Do not fool yourself." The captain smiled, pleased at the spirit of the men. "We know that he is inside the Gulf of Corinth, near a small town called Lepanto."

"How do you know this?"

"Last night Don Juan sent a small scout boat inside the Gulf. Do not think we have a greater force than the enemy. He has nearly three hundred ships and possibly fifty thousand more men."

"The odds are still in our favor," Camillus said carelessly.

The captain grinned. "Well, you are a well-known expert on odds. However, let us not be overconfident."

"We still have the element of surprise," someone volunteered. "He cannot outsail us inside the gulf."

"Let us hope that all their leaders are there," another said. "If we can annihilate them we shall have peace for many years."

"We have found that Ali Pasha, Mohammed Sirocco, Mustapha Pasha, and the Italian renegade Guloudy Ali are all there. It is a bag to capture, I can tell you." The captain blessed himself.

"I should like to run my sword through Guloudy," a soldier said bitterly and there was immediate assent on the part of others.

Famagusta, the last fortress of Cyprus, had been taken by Mustapha Pasha. His promise of clemency had resulted in a massacre of men, women, and children. The Venetian captain, Bragadino, had been flayed alive, his skin stuffed with hay and hung on the bowsprit of his ship. The Christians, enraged at these stories, welcomed combat.

Hot food was served and every effort made to keep the men in spirits as the conflict drew nearer. Captains saw that they were kept busy working on weapons and priests circulated throughout the ships with words of encouragement. The battle had assumed the air of a holy crusade and confidence of help from heaven, besides their splendid armament, raised expectations of victory. Fog crept over the fleet and it grew cooler as the afternoon progressed.

Camillus was not in an easy frame of mind. During the past few days the wound in his leg had started to throb and a sense of deep loneliness came over him. He had just finished an attack of fever that had put him on his back for three weeks and his strength was not fully recovered. He uneasily recalled the prayers he had uttered while ill and so promptly relegated to a forgotten place when well again.

At least, he thought, he had confessed and received the sacraments.

Frustration seemed to have been his lot since the death of his father. At times there had been moments of glory when his work on the field of battle had received meritorious comment but for the most part his existence had become meaningless.

His closest friend, Albrecht Horzen, came over to his side. "Why so glum, Camillus?"

"My leg is bothering me again. Perhaps a little action will liven me up, take my mind off the thought of it."

"It may be that we shall have a stroke of good fortune this very day. Rumor has it that the Turks have a medicine for everything. Possibly we may get one of their doctors as a prisoner and he will cure that wound once and for all."

Camillus laughed. "Be sure and ask every Turk if he is a doctor before you run him through."

A loud shout interrupted the conversation. "A sail! A sail!"

Seamen clambered through the rigging and speedily confirmed the report. A tremendous roar went up from the fleet.

Don Juan ordered the Banner of the League to be raised and from the mizzenpeak of the giant flagship was unfurled the standard, a consecrated cloth of azure damask. The crucifix was embroidered on the upper part while below were the arms of the Church, with those of Spain on the right and those of Venice on the left, united by a chain from which were suspended the arms of Don Juan of Austria.

"This is it."

"Praise be to the Blessed Lord and His Holy Mother."

"God is with us."

A thousand cries rent the air as the vast array of the Ottoman fleet came into view.

Don Juan directed a gun to be fired, the signal for battle.

The noise of the weapon reverberated along the rocky shores of the nearby island. It was Sunday, the memorable seventh of October, fifteen hundred and seventy-one.

The flagship became the center of intense activity. Principal captains of the fleet made hurried visits to the craft, were closeted briefly with Don Juan for final instructions and left to join their own forces.

The Turks moved slowly forward for the wind suddenly veered and blew directly in their faces. Forming a half crescent the great strength of the Ottoman was awe-inspiring but it failed to dampen the ardor of the men of Don Juan.

"I can see jewels from here," Albrecht called to Camillus.

"Loads of them. Every turban has a king's ransom," a Spaniard called.

It was true that the sun shone down on bared Damascus steel and the glint of precious stones in the head coverings of the dark skinned men was visible now but yards away.

"There is Ali Pasha's flagship headed directly for us!"

"You are right!" Captain de Sepolevede shouted, pointing to a great vessel from the mainmast of which floated the outsized banner with thousands of names of the Prophet inscribed upon it.

Both commanders urged their rowers to greater speed and amid the confused roaring of Christian and Turk the two galleys met with a shock that rocked the boats from end to end. A terrific crashing fire of cannon enveloped them in smoke and flame, the barrage of the Spaniards proving much more effective.

Camillus felt rather than saw his companions fall about him. The spirit of the battle was upon him. Calm and collected, he carefully shot Moslems off the prow of their ship. His marksmanship with the arabesque was a byword with his associates.

Arrows and metal flew as thick as leaves in a gale. Almost immediately reserves from other ships arrived to bolster the Pasha. Spaniards fought across the decks and clambered aboard the Moslem vessel where isolated groups waged individual war. The flooring was slippery with blood and cluttered with the grotesque forms of the dead.

Camillus was one of the first aboard the enemy ship and, like the experienced soldier he was, he fought coolly and bitterly. The great sweep of his powerful sword accounted for many of the black bearded men. Don Juan in person had led one of the attacks and Camillus found himself almost at the elbow of the Captain General. Ali Pasha had surged forward and it was the groups of the leaders who waged the fiercest conflict.

An order was issued to release the galley slaves with the promise of freedom if victorious. Don Juan had taken the precaution of having only Spaniards and Italians rowing his galleys and this now stood him in good stead, whereas Ali Pasha had employed captured Christians for his boats. When the Spaniards penetrated to the Moslem holds and broke the chains of the Christian slaves they turned on their masters with a vengeance and augmented the attack with great fury.

Twice the Spaniards were aboard Ali's ship and twice repulsed. Their superb marksmanship and ability with the sword in individual fights proved the decisive factor and once more they surged onto the decks of the infidel and forced him back.

At the crucial moment Ali Pasha was felled and confusion seized his followers. The galley slaves pulled at a mass of twisted figures and dragged forth the fallen form of Ali Pasha, his splendid clothes torn and covered with gore.

"He lives!" one shouted as the Turkish leader twitched and then brushed at his eyes.

Someone threw a bucket of salt water over him and Ali Pasha was helped to his feet.

"You are our prisoner, now," one former slave said, striking the Turk across the face.

"Let us hang him."

"No, give him the whip as we have had it so many times."

"Wait, wait!" The Turk staggered. "I am your prisoner. Bring me to your prince. I shall pay ransom."

Don Juan caught sight of the furor about the green turbaned chief. "Save him!" he shouted. "Bring the Pasha to me!"

He and two of his followers slipped as they started toward the leering captors of the Moslem leader, regaining their feet to see the sweep of a blade decapitate their foremost prisoner. A frenzied shout welled from the throats of the ex-slaves who kicked and beat with feet and weapons at the still form.

"He would have been better a prisoner," Don Juan exclaimed, "but one cannot blame their fury."

The anger of the former slaves was uncontrollable. They stuck the head of Ali Pasha on a pike and raised it aloft for the confused enemy to see. At the same time the green and gold banner inscribed with the thousands of names of Allah was hauled down and the Standard of the League of Christian Princes hoisted to the masthead. The loss of their vaunted leader cast terror into the Turk and suddenly all along the line the Christians forced the fight to victory. Carnage was to be seen on every side, broken cannon, weapons of every sort, sinking ships, and men struggling in the green waters. The decks were littered with the dead and wounded; priests moved about administering the final sacraments.

Back on the *Real,* Camillus leaned against a cabin and sought to regain some of his strength. Miraculously not a scratch was on him although the blood of his opponents splotched his clothing. A hand shook him and he stared into the happy face of Captain de Sepolevede. "Wake up, Camillus," the officer cried. "You were magnificent. I overheard Don Juan ask who you were."

"I must remember that," the other said sarcastically. "What of the others, Horzen, de Fedaris, Calvatti? What of our own band?"

The captain shook his head. "Some of these I have seen but not all. We must trust in God."

The battle had lasted more than four hours and the sky which had been clear now showed threatening clouds. A strong wind buffeted the vessels. The first sign of darkness, the plush velvet of twilight, came creeping in from the east.

The two proud fleets were now a mass of battered and burned hulks, splintered spars, broken masts, shredded canvas, and tilted guns. The sea was littered with wreckage and hundreds clung to whatever support could be had as they desperately attempted to escape the strong hand of the ocean. Dozens of ships blazed and occasional muffled explosions boomed over the water.

High on the masthead of the shell-scarred *Real,* flagship of the Captain General Don Juan, waved the consecrated banner with the Image of Christ looking down upon the carnage created by His children.

CHAPTER VIII

Night swept down swiftly and with it a fierce storm of rain, lightning, and thunder. Rescue work was finally abandoned and the fleet turned for refuge into the neighboring harbor of Petala. Don Juan now called a meeting of all high officers to be held in his quarters.

Resplendent in new uniforms the various leaders greeted their commander with cheers as he emerged from his private cabin. Wine flowed freely with the congratulations bestowed upon each other and all prior petty jealousies were forgotten in this hour of such splendid victory.

"A High Mass of Thanksgiving will be offered in the morning," Don Juan said as he finally held up his hand for silence. "In the order of the day I shall have special prayers of thanks offered to the Blessed Mother for her intercession. We could not have won without such assistance.

"The men have been issued extra rations of wine and food. Arrangements are being made for the wounded to go back to Italy on the fastest vessel. All other ships will be repaired here. I am now anxious to hear any suggestions from you, gentlemen."

"What else is to be done, Don Juan?" Andria Doria smiled. "You have thought of everything."

"It is most kind of you to say that, Admiral. However, there is one thing we must do. I want two men from each ship to be signalized for valor and brought before me as soon as possible. I want to thank them personally and bestow a small token of my esteem. Now, mind you, gentlemen, these men must have been outstanding and please do not overlook this because of any personal traits you may not like in them. This gesture will be an incentive to all others so you must pick the proper men."

Thus it was that Captain de Sepolevede came forward to the deck where Camillus lolled in the company of his depleted band. "De Lellis, Horzen!" he called, and the two, startled, came to their feet.

"What is it now, Captain? Do not tell us that we are to personally invade Turkey," Horzen said, his eyes sparkling beneath a roughly bandaged forehead.

"It has been difficult for me to make this decision," the officer replied. "Don Juan has ordered each leader to select two men for his personal recognition. I wish I could pick all of you but the orders are clear. You, De Lellis, step forward. Horzen, you are also my choice. Come with me, now."

"To Don Juan?" Horzen asked. "We are not too presentable."

Camillus stared at his companion. "You are a fool, Horzen," he said. "If we are dirty and soiled it has been in Don Juan's service. As for selecting me, Captain, you could do otherwise. I do not care for fair words. All of these men have done as much and perhaps more than I. Make a better choice and please us all."

"You are a cool one, De Lellis, and may I say, a most insolent one. I have made up my mind. You two are to follow me and this is an order."

Camillus towered head and shoulders over the assemblage of brilliantly arrayed men gathered around the commander. The crown of his head was but inches from the low ceiling and many eyes were upon him as he was presented.

"De Lellis," Don Juan said. "It is a noble name. May I ask from whence you come?"

"Bucchianico, the Province of Abruzzo in Italy, your excellency."

"Ah, it is small wonder that you are an excellent soldier." Don Juan smiled. "The Abruzzesi are the descendants of the hardy Samnites who refused the Roman conquest."

"I have heard the legend, excellency." Camillus was pleased. "My mother's family is of them. My father's, the De Lellis clan, have lived in Abruzzo for a thousand years. They are of the Roman line of the Laelii."

"You have carried their name well this day."

"I have trained under the instructions of my late father, Don Juan de Lellis," Camillus said proudly.

"That is why I thought I recognized him," one spoke from the group. "You have the same bearing, young man."

"You knew the father, Don Carlos?" the commander in chief asked.

"It was my good fortune to have had him in my service. He was truly a great soldier and it is apparent that his son has inherited his father's noble qualities."

"Thank you, sir." Camillus bowed.

"You are carrying well the tradition of your family." Don Juan took two small bags from the table. "Here is a slight trifle, a good will gesture for your outstanding services. What you have done today cannot be repaid in gold."

"Thank you, Excellency."

"We have our eyes on soldiers such as you two," the commander continued. "You will not be forgotten."

Horzen turned excitedly as they once more reached the deck. "You are a marked man, Camillus. It would do you well to stay in the service of Don Juan."

"You, too, are as marked as I," Camillus returned. "We shall see what those fine words mean. It was good, however, to hear praise of my father."

His mind went back to the lonely inn where his father had died, attended only by himself and a country priest. He knew that the honors accorded the old soldier had meant nothing in that final hour and his own immediate recognition had not impressed him. He felt the old unrest enter his mind but he immediately banished it.

"It does not matter how they think now, my dear Horzen." He hefted the bag of coin. "This is what matters. This is what counts. Their fine words do not buy us anything but this — this has power."

The other grinned. "I have always liked it. We shall have a much better time ashore with it than without."

"Ashore? We shall have a better time right here on the ship, my fine friend. We have good stakes to play."

"Play?"

"Cards. Dice. You are not stupid. You must understand that we are in business with such a hoard of coin. We can pool our money and no one in the fleet will be able to beat us."

Horzen shook his head doubtfully. "I do not think we should play, Camillus. It is against the orders of the Captain General. It means trouble."

"Do not be so foolish, Albrecht. We are sitting in a fine spot. We have made a name for ourselves. You do not think anyone will stop us? The bars will be let down. The battle is over. This had always been so and you know it."

"After all, I should like to see an order to that effect."

"You talk like a peasant and not a soldier. Come, rely upon me. We shall arrange a game. If you have any courage other than what you use in battle now is the time to show it."

Two hours later De Lellis and Horzen stood once more before Don Juan but in a different capacity. Tiberio, a close friend and two other soldiers caught in the card game, were standing with them.

Don Juan looked coldly at De Lellis and Horzen. "You two quickly made use of your prize money to incite gambling. Is this not so?"

"It is my fault, Excellency," Camillus said with no deference. "My companion had nothing to do with it. I thought that the victory called for a little celebration. I did not think such strict regulations would be maintained."

"It is for me to decide what shall and shall not be done," Don Juan replied, the tone of the other's voice not lost to him. "You will both receive full punishment. I had hopes that those I recognized for special honors would be examples to the rest of the men. You two, alone, have proved me wrong. You have taken the opportunity to break one of my most rigid rules. You have flaunted my orders. I will not tolerate this disobedience."

He turned to Horzen. "At least you show regret for your actions." He paused and turned to Camillus. "Apparently there is nothing in your make-up that calls for remorse. The ship carrying the wounded back to Italy is leaving within the hour. Get your gear and go aboard. You will be paid off at the docking of the ship. You are no more a part of my force. The others are not so guilty but they must also go. It will teach you that obedience comes before all else."

"I have said that I alone am guilty," Camillus offered.

"It is not enough for me," Don Juan replied.

"Then take this, for I want no part of it." De Lellis threw his bag of gold to the table.

There was a gasp from the assembled officers. Don Juan paled but remained calm. "You are insolent but I will overlook it," he said, picking up the coin and handing it to an aide. "Give this to the first man you meet outside the door. Go now."

He looked at Camillus de Lellis. "Just one more word, my young soldier," he said coldly. "You had better watch yourself or soon you will find that you are not so self-sufficient as you think. Go, at once."

Camillus was trembling with anger as he left the cabin.

CHAPTER IX

After his dismissal by Don Juan, Camillus and his companions were landed at Naples. Albrecht Horzen, remorseful, lost no time in making a decision to forego future military work. "I am a carpenter and painter," he told Camillus. "This soldier life is no more for me. I am going back to the hammer and brush."

"You sound like an artist," De Lellis scoffed. "I have told you that I already have the promise of Captain de Sepolevede that his brother, the commandant of a garrison twenty miles from here, will hire us."

"No." The other shook his head. "For the past twelve years I have wandered from one place to the other. I am growing old. You are a young man."

"And you are a stupid one," Camillus said, and then relented. "I am sorry, Albrecht. It is only that I am upset at losing such a good friend. I cannot forget that you have been my close companion, that you nursed me back to life at Corfu."

Horzen smiled. "Only what you would have done for me. But you are not alone, Camillus. You have Tiberio, Federico, and Angelo."

"Federico and Angelo are not going with us," Camillus said gloomily. "Tiberio needs you as well as me to look after him. He is helpless, as you well know."

"Only when he is drinking and he loves you, Camillus."

"As we do him. Oh, well." Camillus stood up. "Let us

hope that we will meet again. You know that you may depend upon me."

"That I do. It could be that we may meet again someday. I know that neither of us will fail the other."

Camillus found little difficulty in hiring out his sword during the hectic years from 1571 through 1574. In rapid succession he passed from the services of Philip II of Spain, the Duke of Venice, and a number of minor princes into the audacious band of one Fabio, the foremost soldier of fortune of that era.

Gambling was still his predominant passion and although money came in large quantities it was soon dissipated across the gaming tables of a dozen nations. At Palermo he had lost his entire savings, a considerable sum, and once at Naples he lost everything, including his shirt, so that he had to take it off in the very street to pay his wager. All during this time Tiberio was with him, a good-natured, lovable man with as strong an addiction to drink and brawling as Camillus had for gambling. A stalwart bond grew between them and what belonged to one was also the property of the other.

In November of 1574 they found themselves once more in Naples, in one of the low haunts near the waterfront. Camillus had suffered little from his leg wound and, although fear still assailed him when he thought of it, for the most part his ailment had become a minor matter. His principal occupation was fighting and gambling and living a riotous life.

The wine cellar was not the cleanest in the great, sprawling city of Naples. Neither was it the dirtiest but it did not come far from that distinction. Unwashed bodies, spicy food, and the dregs of stale wine filled the air with an almost sodden heaviness.

The man behind the counter, tapping the casks, could have demonstrated, by use of his apron, the color of every vintage for years past. His assistant, apparently his wife, judging from her manner, was just as unkempt. Her only claim to cleanliness was a starched house cap that rode like a pure beacon on a sea of disordered and straggling black waves.

The late, hot sun, slanting through the barred windows, cast patterns across the dirty floor, scarred tables, and strange faces of the place. Cards and dice lay scattered across the largest board and six men, with glum faces barely hiding antagonism toward the seventh, watched him rake in a small pile of coins. "It is finished. You have taken everything."

Camillus de Lellis laughed as he put the money in his pouch. "It did not take long. You were waiting, my chickens, to be plucked. Come." He snapped his fingers at the owner. "Wine all around and keep it coming."

The countenance of his late opponents brightened. "We shall have at least a drink for our money."

The soldier laughed. "You may have everything you wish, except my money."

"If you are as victorious on the field of battle as at the gaming table you should go far."

"It is not too bad to lose to a gentleman."

"Thank you, thank you. You have helped me much, my friends. I shall now buy a horse, thanks to your generosity, and shall go looking for another patron."

"What of your friend?" One of them indicated a figure in dirty, military attire stretched out on a nearby bench. "The wine did not agree with him."

"Tiberio," Camillus shouted but the only response was a mutter. "I shall take good care of my friend, do not worry." He turned to the others. "What is mine is his. That is the code of our companionship."

"I envy you soldiers," one said. "You lead a fine life with glory all around; wine, women, fighting."

"Do not talk so foolishly. It is a good life but it is not without hardship and danger. One must be born to it. There is as much wine, women, and fighting in the streets of Naples. As for me, give me wine and fighting. They are sufficient."

"Hardship seems to agree with you. You look very healthy."

"Appearances are deceitful, my friend. All has not been easy for me. You would not think that but a short time ago I lay starving or that I have almost died of the dysentery. You would not think that I have seen my comrades so famished they would rip open the stomachs of dead Turks and eat their livers."

They stared at him in openmouthed horror. "So God spared you to teach us gambling."

A shadow passed over Camillus' face but he did not reply and contented himself with draining the goblet. "More wine."

"It is too bad that Vittorio Aggate is not here," the woman said as she poured the liquid.

"Vittorio Aggate? Who is he?" Camillus asked.

"He is a thief," said one of the men.

"You had better watch your tongue, Sebastian. Vittorio is very quick with the knife."

"Why is it then that Vittorio always wins if he is not a thief?"

"No man always wins," Camillus remarked.

"You do not know Vittorio," the woman said.

The soldier laughed. "I have known many Vittorios."

"But not Vittorio Aggate." A calm, assured voice said this from the doorway.

"Vittorio!" the woman cried, and was echoed by her husband.

"Listen, my friend," one of the men at the table whispered to Camillus. "You had better leave. This Vittorio is in league with the devil. He always appears when one has won at cards or dice and in a little while he has all the money. He cannot lose."

"Then he is in league with the owner and a messenger is what brings him here," Camillus replied and turned to the newcomer.

His clothes were in violent contrast to the poor ones of the patrons, his manner arrogant, a patronizing smile upon a face almost effeminate were it not for the sharp, black eyes that shone like glass.

"Good day to you, Signor. You are the gambler that I have been waiting for," Camillus said. "I have cleaned your friends of all their funds. Would you like to join them?"

The newcomer did not at once reply but walked slowly to the table and sat down, still studying the soldier's face.

"If it is your wish, my friend. I do play at cards, dice, or what you will in the way of chance."

A laugh went up from the others. Camillus felt an instant dislike for this dandefied stranger and wanted nothing more than to trounce him not only at cards but physically. "Let us play," he said harshly.

The soldier on the setee sat up and then hastily crossed the room with weaving steps.

"Oh, ho, Tiberio, you are awake."

"Let us leave, Camillus. You have enough money to outfit three men now. Do not chance losing it."

"What? We shall not leave more than we have, Tiberio, my good friend. I shall outfit you from head to foot with the best of equipment. You just go over there and sit down. I shall attend to this business. Here." He thrust a bottle into his friend's hand and Tiberio shuffled to a distant table to drink himself once more to sleep.

"What shall we play?" Camillus asked.

"It does not matter to me. They are all the same."

"I am not used to an answer like that." Camillus stared at Vittorio and was further ruffled by the other's attitude. "I asked you a question and I will have an answer."

"I am sorry, Signor. I was extending you your choice. Shall we play at dice?"

"That is more like it," Camillus said. "First, we shall all have some wine."

The game that ensued was a topic of conversation for many months. Those privileged to witness it were anxious to recount the tale to all who would listen. It was a definite match of men who knew gambling, chances, odds, and every trick.

Camillus found himself opposed by a man the like of whom he had not seen handle dice since the days of the late Don Juan de Lellis. It was not long before the feeling crowded upon him that the player across the table could not be beaten. It was not his nature to yield and he fought back with all the skill the years had given him.

"He must be the devil," Camillus thought as the man made runs that seemed impossible. He examined the dice closely.

"I shall be happy to use other dice," his opponent said mildly. "Perhaps you would like to play some other game?"

"No, no. These will do."

Camillus watched the other's pile of coins grow steadily larger. It soon became apparent to all that he simply could not win and in a series of amazing runs Vittorio made this an established fact. He raked in the last pot and glanced at his opponent. Camillus had been reduced to putting up his sword, dagger, powder flask, and coat. He now sat, half dressed, staring at this man who had so shattered his fortunes in such a short time.

"I have nothing left," he said.

One of the onlookers giggled. "How about your shoes?"

A flash of anger came over the young soldier. "I should have taken yours."

"But you would only have lost them to Aggate." The speaker shrugged.

The young giant stood up, his brawny arms revealed by the shortness of his inside shirt. He was keenly aware of the amusement on faces about him and bitterly regretted his continuance of play.

Tiberio stirred as Camillus shook him and then sat upright. "Ah, you have finished." He looked closer. "But why are you dressed like this?"

"I have lost all. It is nothing. A few years ago I lost my very shirt in this city. It is evil luck for me to play in Naples. Come, let us get out of here."

"You have lost? That is impossible. What are we to do?"

"Let us get out of here!" Camillus said savagely, helping his stupefied friend to his feet and heading for the stairs. Silence was upon the room as they made the ascent, Tiberio almost falling. Camillus de Lellis did not know it but when the door of the low drinking place closed after him it also closed over his tumultuous gambling career. He was never to touch cards or dice again.

CHAPTER X

Shafts of sunlight bathed the street in brightness and Camillus blinked his eyes. It was a poor section yet everybody within view seemed happy. Some children playing at a hop and skip game paused, their gleeful voices dying at sight of the two men. They gazed in wonderment at the half-dressed condition of the young giant and the befuddled actions of his companion.

"Let us get out of here," Camillus said bitterly as the youngsters crowded around.

"Where are your clothes?" one, bolder than the rest, shouted. Immediately the others took up the chorus.

"They're drunk soldiers without clothes."

"Hey, look at the drunk soldiers. Drunk, drunk, drunk."

Camillus hastened his steps, one strong arm holding Tiberio up. They were followed for a few blocks, the cries of the children attracting the curious stares of older people, but soon were out of the vicinity and Camillus propped his companion against a building.

"Have you any money at all?" he asked impatiently.

"None, I swear it, Camillus. You know that you have been paying my way."

"Your clothes are rags, not worth selling." Camillus was disgusted at the frayed and dirty apparel.

"But they cover me," Tiberio said with drunken solemnity.

"You had better get some clothes. It will be cold tonight. You had better get some clothes."

"Silence!" Camillus said. "You are more of a fool than I thought," he added bitterly, "yet you are not half the fool that I am."

"It would be good to have some food," Tiberio remarked. "You know we have been drinking all day, Camillus. We need food."

"You need a good beating," his companion said savagely, shaking him. "Come, let us walk. Perhaps it will sober you enough to give me some sensible replies."

The urge to keep moving dominated Camillus for he was now feeling the main reaction to his losses. His nerves were also suffering from the wine which had been the main part of his diet for the past few days. It came to him suddenly that he was hungry and he noted with foreboding that the sun would soon be set. They walked until they came to a plaza where Tiberio insisted that they sit down on a bench and rest.

"What are we to do?" he wailed. "No one knows us in this terrible city and we are without funds. We will surely starve, Camillus."

"You are too fat. It will take a lot of starving."

"It is a poor time to jest. Ah, I have it." Tiberio's face lighted with a smile. "Let us go to the door of a church and ask for the priest. We will tell him our story and he will at least feed us."

Camillus found his anger increasing at the ramblings of his friend. "You do just that," he cried. "Go now and beg for your stomach. As for me I shall sit here and think. If you wish to see me I shall still be here. Go and give me some peace."

"I should like to have you with me." Tiberio stood up. "You look really desperate, Camillus, half clothed as you are."

"Get out!" the giant shouted in a sudden rage. "Get away from me, you idiot. This is where I will meet you after you have fed your gluttonous stomach."

Tiberio had seen instances of his friend's wrath before and backed away. "I shall look for you here," he said hastily and hurried down the street.

Camillus now felt the fury in his heart directed at his own condition, knowing that he, alone, was to blame. "Where can I go for a night's sleep? Where can I get at least some bread? I must have money to buy something to cover me." The thoughts pounded in his head.

Across the plaza lights burned in shops and houses and it came suddenly to Camillus that the sun would be gone within a matter of minutes. Already a fresh breeze whipped across the open space and he shivered. Memories of his recent fever returned to alarm him. "It would be the end if I were to become ill. I should surely die."

His eyes caught the outline of a huge church at one end of the plaza. "Ah, I shall go there and at least rest. There will be no wind and maybe I shall have an idea."

He hurried toward the building and quickly entered. It was cool but not cold and he sank upon one of the benches at the rear. Stretching himself, he was suddenly conscious of a sharp pain that ran from his ankle to the calf of his left leg. Fear gripped him as he recalled his ailment and recognized this as one of the warnings that it might return.

"It cannot be the wound. It has not bothered me for two years." He tried to allay his alarm. "I must have walked for miles. Oh, what a situation I am in and there is no one I can turn to for help."

"It is at least warmer here than outside. The wind must have chilled me." He thought bitterly of Vittorio and would have cursed him if he had been anywhere but in church.

Seasoned campaigner that he was, Camillus stretched out on the long bench and cradled his face in his arms. Sleep that he had consistently neglected of late, as long as he had had money to spend, crept in and claimed his exhausted frame.

When he awakened he heard noises from the street. Dull gray streamed through the high windows and Camillus sat up with a start. "I must have slept the night through," he exclaimed and found that he ached all over. His leg was now stiff and he was forced to stamp on the stone floor to awaken the circulation. When it commenced he again felt the twinge of nagging pain and he muttered bitterly. "That is all I need. I am faint from hunger." He walked to the door and wondered if Tiberio had returned the previous night.

People were starting to enter the church and Camillus stood half hidden by a door and watched them. The bell in the tower was ringing and he knew that Mass would shortly begin. He left the main portal and stopped on the top step.

"Charity, a few coins, young master," a trembling voice reached his ears and he looked at the forlorn face of an ancient woman in rags. Farther down the steps stood two more beggars, a man and a woman, crying out to those entering the church.

Camillus unconsciously reached for his wallet and suddenly the icy hand of terror gripped him and he trembled as he recalled yesterday's disaster.

"One small coin, kind sir."

He looked at the woman. A feeling of pity ran through him at sight of her rags and filth. "I have nothing or I would give you something. I, too, am penniless," he said bitterly.

"You are big and strong. Do not beg here." Her wheedling tones changed to shrill peevishness. "This is my place. The top step has been my place for years."

Anger and shame raced through him. "I am not here to beg," he said haughtily. "I am but coming from the church." He brushed by and was aware of her continued accusation and warning as he went down the steps and hurried away.

The more he walked the more pain tortured his leg. He rolled down his stocking and breathed an oath. There was a slight, red swelling. "It is starting again. God, what shall I do? I have nothing." His desperate mind repeated the endless question.

He kept walking, almost in a frenzy. The food in shops tempted him but after the first few pauses before enticing displays he banished them from his mind and kept up his hurried walk. He walked for hours until finally the pain increased in his leg so that he was forced to stop and rest on a plaza bench.

There was a fountain nearby and he slaked his thirst with great gulps. "If only I could meet someone I know, but there are so few friends in this cursed place. I do not know where to find anyone."

He stood watching the passing people. "They are all different," he said. "Yet every one of them has a home."

Memories of his father and mother swirled about him and his desolation increased. Some people looked quizzically at him and he did not stop long in any one place. He crossed before a church and noticed, spaced at regular intervals, men and women in rags, crying out to those who entered. "I would rather starve than that," he muttered and stopped to watch. He marveled at the generosity of churchgoers who hardly ever passed a supplicant.

"I must have food," he muttered, feeling faint and slightly dizzy.

A coin was thrust into his hand and he looked at it with dazed eyes. The donor was disappearing within the church but hunger now gripped the young giant and he knew that he could not call out and refuse the money. Instead he stood there and to his astonishment, within the space of a few minutes, had almost a handful of coin. The other beggars gazed at his great frame with soured eyes and muttering but Camillus paid no heed to them. "I have enough to buy some cheese and bread," he exclaimed and left the steps, his destination a store whose contents had almost driven him to desperation a short time before.

"Bread, bread and some cheese," he cried in his loud voice as he went through the door of the store regardless of the half dozen customers already waiting. They stared in astonishment at the half clothed giant throwing coins to the counter and shouldering them aside.

The fat proprietor looked at him coldly. "There are others before you," he said, his eyes appraising the scanty attire.

Rage coursed through the hungry frame of Camillus. "You dog!" he shouted, clamping his hand to his side and finding no sword. "Give me bread and cheese now or I will stick you."

So fierce was his demeanor that the man backed away. All conversation had stopped and those near to Camillus retreated and gazed with pity upon the pale face of the proprietor.

"But how much cheese? I do not know," the man sputtered.

"There is the money. You have spent a lifetime counting money, weighing cheese, and cheating people," Camillus shouted. "Give me all that the money will buy."

The man trembled into action and hastily selected a long loaf and a sizable wedge of cheese not weighed and put them on the counter.

Before he could utter another word Camillus snatched the loaf and tore a great hunk from it with his teeth, at the same time breaking the cheese and cramming some of it into his mouth. He chewed with great vigor and intensity and then only was he aware of the sudden silence that had descended upon the shop. He glared at those about him, grabbed the remainder of the cheese, and hurried through the door.

"He must be mad," the owner stuttered.

"Bah. He is a beggar and the biggest one I have ever seen," one customer volunteered. "He has been on the church steps shouting for alms. I saw him."

"A beggar is he?" the owner said. "He should be locked up or, better still, put in a galley and made to work. I shall handle him well if he dares to show his ugly self around here in the future. So he is a beggar, eh?"

Camillus put as much distance as possible between himself and the shop, all the while eating the bread and cheese but feeling a burning indignity attack his pride. "What a low level I have descended to," he thought. "What would my proud father say? I have disgraced the name of De Lellis."

He brushed the last crumb from his bristling cheeks and physically felt much better. "I never knew food could be so good." He stared around and did not recognize the neighborhood.

"I am lost again." He thought of his predicament and suddenly the events of the past few hours crowded upon him and he felt waves of shame. "I had to eat," he said sullenly but it did not stop the emotions that gripped him.

He leaned against a tree and wept. "What is to become of me? There is no one that I can turn to except in the guise of a beggar." He thought of his mother and his boyhood home and the gentry that had often visited there. "I have descended lower than any of my ancestors," he cried. "It would have been better to die at Corfu than to be reduced to this situation. Can no one help to save what little honest pride I must still retain?"

He thought of God, but God meant obedience and that

was a trait he lacked except under military compulsion and even then it was none too certain. He thought of God as giving and not receiving.

"How many times have I tossed a gold or silver coin to some cringing beggar and now I am one of them. God help me — but He will not. Why should He? I am doomed."

Weariness had almost overcome him and his hunger was not fully abated. To add to his discomfort a soft rain started to fall and he looked about for refuge. He caught sight of an ancient church down the street and hurried toward it. "It is a good thing people believe in religion or else I would have no place to go," he thought as he climbed the stairs and entered.

CHAPTER XI

The calmness of the interior soothed him and he sank gratefully to a bench. Confusion reigned in his mind and he was trembling as he stretched out his legs and stared at the distant altar and the dim light that burned before the sanctuary.

"God, if you are listening to me why is it that I must be reduced to such a situation?" He felt ashamed at his involuntary prayer, knowing that he had previously paid little attention to the supernatural. He almost laughed as he thought of his remarks to his uncle, the priest, about joining the Franciscans.

"It is only that I wanted something to hold on to," he declared. "What effrontery for me to think of God and ask His help after the miserable life I have led. There is no one to care for me. I am doomed in this life and the next and deserve both."

He stared at the altar, his mind again going back to his boyhood days. The huge crucifix suspended from one wall fascinated him and he stared at length, almost believing that the figure moved.

"I must be going mad," he whispered and was conscious again of the ache in his leg. "I will die from this," he muttered bitterly. "I am no good as a soldier if that accursed wound returns to me."

St. Giacomo Hospital came to mind. "If I could walk to Rome they might take me back." But he dismissed the idea. He had left a mark which the authorities at the hospital could not easily forget. "Perhaps it is just as well. I could not stand that place with the evil attendants. Hospitals are places to die."

Likelihood of employment seemed remote, knowing as he did that all his life he had done nothing but soldiering. "Who will have a soldier with no armor and no clothes? Then I am afraid that this leg will bother me. What am I to do?"

Despair crowded upon Camillus and in a sudden frenzy he leaped to his feet and ran out of the door coming face to face with a well dressed, middle aged man who paused in some consternation at the wild glare in the youth's eyes. "He has money." The thought flashed in the mind of Camillus, his gaze roving to the leather wallet at the man's belt, but he quickly rejected the idea with a rush of shame.

He stood directly in the path of the man, who asked in a kindly tone, "You are in need of help, my son?"

Camillus could have suddenly wept. "Very much so, sir, to my shame." He choked upon the words.

The man reached into the bag, extracted a fistful of coins, and put them in the hand of Camillus.

"This is too much, sir."

"In God's name get yourself a cloak. You come from a good place, the church. Be of courage. Your prayers will be answered." The man passed into the building.

Camillus descended the stairs, his mind in a whirl, and set out across the park where a familiar figure lounged on a bench. "Tiberio!" he cried. "Where have you been? You did not return last night."

"But I did and you were not here." His friend added with shame, "I had money but it is gone. You apparently have not fared well. Have you any food?"

"Some. Have you any? Have you any money?"

"Nothing. There is not work to be had, either."

"Work? What kind of work would you have me believe you have tried to get?"

"Well, I looked around to see if anyone needed recruits," Tiberio replied.

"You are not telling the truth," Camillus said sternly. "Come, I have money. We shall eat but I must have some of this coin to buy a cloak."

"Wonderful news!" Tiberio laughed happily. "Camillus, I know where there is a game. Perhaps your luck will be with you and we can wait for the food and the cloak."

Camillus stared at his friend and noted for the first time that his belt and dagger were gone. "You are a rogue, Tiberio. You have sold the last of your equipment and you have been drunk. You are likewise a fool if you think I am going hungry and unclothed to lose my money at gambling."

"This cannot be you, Camillus. You have never refused a game."

"I am refusing it now," Camillus said firmly. "It is not that I would not like to play but I must have a cloak and some food. You are welcome to come with me."

"I never thought that I would hear you say that anything was more important than cards or dice."

Camillus felt a surge of anger. "You must have just filled your belly with food, you idiot, to talk that way to me. I am starving and I am cold. Do you know how I got this money, do you?" He almost shouted in a sudden rage.

"Did you find it?" Tiberio asked timidly, having great respect for the other's anger and knowing what it could lead to.

"Did I find it, you dolt!" Camillus shouted so that a few people passing by turned to look. "I begged it. I, Camillus de

Lellis, begged it. Now, you fool, will you come along and keep your babbling to yourself?"

Tiberio followed him into a shop where after much haggling and threatening Camillus succeeded in obtaining a cloak somewhat short for him.

"It is a wonderful fit." The shop owner rubbed his palms together. "It was made for you. Yes, it is a beautiful fit."

"Say that again," Camillus said menacingly. "Say it but once more, you thief, and I will stuff it down your lying throat."

"Now, now, Camillus," Tiberio intervened.

"Quiet!"

"I was only trying to please, Your Excellency," the man whined.

"Bah!" Camillus threw the required money to the counter, wrapped the garment about him, and swaggered from the place.

"It does look good," Tiberio said timidly.

"Mention the cloak again and you will regret it," Camillus threatened. "Now, let us eat."

They ate well that day and also the next, sleeping in churches for the night. The next day the money was gone. "You will have to do as I do," Camillus said to his companion as they stopped before a church.

"I cannot beg," Tiberio declared.

"Then you cannot eat what I beg. Beg or starve. It is all the same to me." Camillus took his stand on the top step and immediately a dirty, evil looking man accosted him. "You are in my place, big one," he said in a slow voice.

"I did not know you were the pastor," Camillus retorted. "Get away from me or I will break your head."

"He is a devil with the knife, big man," an old crone cried from the lowest step.

"Why, you dirty old hag." The evil-looking man went down the steps and hit the old lady, pushing her along the walk. "Get out of my sight. Do not ever come near me."

Camillus, suffused with a towering rage, leaped the steps, snatched up a crutch another beggar had placed on the ground and belabored the man with swinging blows. "You dog, hitting a lady. I will teach you some manners."

The man, astounded at the unexpected assault, tried to crowd in on the giant as he suddenly flashed open a knife, but a rapid succession of lusty blows sent him into the gutter. Camillus continued to beat him.

A crowd was rapidly gathering and suddenly Tiberio grasped his infuriated friend by the arm and pointed down the street where three men were approaching on the run. "We must go. The police are coming!" Tiberio shouted in terror.

"Let the beggars fight," one onlooker cried.

"Yes, do not interfere," another called.

"We will be thrown in jail, put in the galleys!" Tiberio shrieked and set off down the street.

Camillus dealt one more telling blow on the prostrate man and then ran after his fleeing companion. They were spurred on to greater speed by wild yelling and they looked back to see a small group in pursuit. "Faster, faster!" Camillus drew alongside Tiberio and swiftly, grimly, they increased their lead.

Finally they stopped. They were on a long road and no one was in sight. Tiberio dropped in exhaustion upon a rock, sweat rolling down his face, his chest heaving from the exercise. He glanced at his companion who seemed to show no great physical effects from the chase. "Why did you do that? Do you know that we almost landed in prison?" he cried as soon as his tortured lungs would permit.

"Do not question me!" Camillus shouted. "If we are hunted, get up off your fat haunches and let us move out of this devil's own place." He yanked Tiberio to his feet and propelled him forward.

That was the beginning of travel that brought the pair through many towns and cities. They resorted to the only method they knew to obtain money, begging at farm doors, churches, and wherever the chance offered a meal or a few coins.

"It is not such a bad living," Tiberio said one night as they bedded down in a haystack.

"You are a fool." Camillus was angry. "Do you think I would do nothing else if I could? I cannot starve but do not tell me it is a good life."

"I meant no harm."

"Well, then, keep your platitudes to yourself. We are beggars. Make no mistake about it. We may die beggars."

"It is better than most jobs."

"You never had a job and this is not one. How do you know what work is outside of the army? I would work if I knew what to work at. Who would hire us? We are dirty and certainly evil looking. I have no desire to beg and I do not look upon it as a good job as you do. Now keep your silence while I think."

Their clothes had become tattered and one glance betrayed their station. Never did they have enough money to refurnish their wardrobe and begging only gave them sufficient money to eat.

Tiberio was happy but Camillus grew more despondent. The constant exercise of walking had driven all pain from his legs and the only ills he now felt were the pangs of hunger which came too often. "We shall never have enough money to buy equipment," he constantly lamented.

"If we could but meet with some of our old commanders we would not need money for equipment. They would fit us out. Let us go and seek out some of them," Tiberio had suggested.

"Do you think that I, Camillus de Lellis, would appear before my former comrades in this filthy outfit?"

Tiberio shrugged and the begging continued.

Occasionally word of some expedition reached them and it was then that the young giant was most difficult to live with or even tolerate. He tortured himself with all kinds of ideas and then fell back into the black depths of despondency.

One night Camillus made up his mind. "We are not far from Barletta," he said. "We must go there and get equipment money. We will never be able to buy anything unless we work. If we do not have equipment and join some group we will surely die beggars. Is that what you want, Tiberio?"

"Can we get work?"

"We can try. Did you not hear today that there is a war in Dalmatia? All that we need are passable outfits. We can do it. I am going to try. Are you with me?"

In the autumn of 1574 they came into the town of Manfredonia. They were without funds and selected a likely looking street on which to solicit aid.

"Let us meet here within two hours," Camillus said, and they went their separate ways. A cathedral loomed in his view and he immediately dispensed with the idea of house to house begging and made his way toward the church.

The day was raw, the sky gray, overcast with shadows, the wind biting and cold. Camillus shivered and silently cursed the weather that caused the devoted to hurry into the church, clutching cloaks about them, loath to pause even in the name of charity.

"At this rate I will not get enough money to eat, let alone

buy equipment," he muttered. He longed for the warmth of a wineshop and the tingling heat of a drink.

"Pickings are no good today, brother."

Camillus stared at the speaker, a fellow petitioner, his clothes even in worse condition than his own, "Be off with you," he said roughly. "Why don't you go to the other door? You are driving my patrons from me."

"Oh, so you have patrons?"

"I'll patron you." Camillus glared fiercely and the other immediately retreated.

People continued to pass through the doors and then there came a pause. The sound of music issued from the church. "Mass has started," Camillus thought. "The latecomers are always in too much of a hurry to give. I will have to get in out of the cold until the services are over."

He was about to enter when a carriage stopped at the curb and an elderly gentleman alighted. Camillus immediately turned and waited, his hopes once more rising. "Have you a small coin, for the love of charity, sir?" he cried in a high voice as the man, with difficulty, ascended the stairs.

The newcomer had sharp eyes in a ruddy face and he turned them upon Camillus. "Ah, I have seen you before," he declared. "Yes, I marked your size. You were at a church door in Naples a few months ago. Were you not?"

Camillus had always found it difficult to lie. Rather he was addicted to vociferously declaring himself upon a point regardless of the consequences. "I have traveled from town to town, sir. There is no work for me. Yes, you could have seen me in Naples for I am in reduced circumstances and have stood at other church doors."

Camillus did not realize it but he was engaged in what later he knew had been the most important conversation in his whole life.

S T .   C A M I L L U S / 87

CHAPTER XII

The man was silent but his gaze continued to rest upon the giant.

"What is the matter with this man?" Camillus began to grow furious. "Must I be interrogated for want of a pittance? I shall tell him so."

The man took a wallet from his pouch and Camillus' hopes soared. "I will give you money to buy yourself food but that is not all. You are big and strong. You could work."

"Why, yes, if I could get it." Camillus was taken aback. "No one will hire a soldier without equipment."

"There is other work beside the military," the man said mildly. "Have you any objections to hard work?"

"Hard work?" Camillus said blankly. "I have done my share while serving. No, I am not afraid of work."

"We should thank God for work. You shall have something to do." He took a handful of silver and gave it to Camillus.

"Thank you, thank you, sir."

Camillus was about to move away when the little man placed a hand on his arm. "I have told you that I will get you work and so I shall. I do not think a man of your physique should be reduced to begging. You are a young man."

"I am twenty-four, sir." Camillus was anxious to be away.

"Ah, to be that age again. Listen, my son. You go and get a good meal with that money that God was so kind to let me have for you. You will then go to the Capuchin Monastery outside this town. Anyone will direct you. Ask for the Prior and tell him that Antonio Di Nicastro has sent you there to work. You will not be refused."

"Antonio Di Nicastro," Camillus repeated, fervently wishing the man would go into the church. "I shall remember it. Thank you again, sir."

"Here." The man reached into his pouch and handed Camillus a card. "My address is on this. If you have difficulty you must come to see me and I will go with you."

Camillus watched him pass into the church, then quickly counted the money, much more than he needed for his immediate hunger. "I am in luck but I had better not meet him again," he said as he hurried away. "Ah — " he stopped. "I do recall him. He told me to buy a cloak in Naples. Well, I did buy the cloak. He is a very charitable man."

Seated in a small shop he hastily devoured bread, sausage, and cheese with liberal helpings of wine. Then he sat back. Outside the rain was now beating against the window and Camillus felt warm and somewhat at ease. He searched the street for Tiberio as their meeting place was in front of the food shop.

"You have done well today," the owner said slyly as he saw him counting the remainder of the money.

"And so too have you," Camillus said angrily.

The man shrugged and looked up as the door opened and Tiberio came in, his garments dripping.

He glanced at the empty dishes before his friend. "At least you have fared well enough to eat," he said bitterly, "Not a scudi from the people for all of my whining."

"Give my friend the same that I had," Camillus called to the shopkeeper and watched with satisfaction as Tiberio literally tore into the food.

Tiberio finally finished. "Oh, you are a jewel," he said. "You are always most generous, Camillus. Where did you get such luck?"

"Luck? If I had luck would I be in such a position as this? No, Tiberio, I met a man who had seen me in Naples." He eyed his friend. "He promised me work. You must come with me and I shall ask for you also."

"Work!" Tiberio exclaimed. "Did you say work?"

"You have never done any of it but there is such a thing. Yes, I have told you the truth."

"What kind of work?"

"How do I know what kind of work?" Camillus said impatiently. "All I know is that I was told it would be hard work. I am to go to the Capuchin Monastery outside of town and ask for the Prior and tell him that Antonio Di Nicastro sent me."

"Capuchin Monastery. You are crazy, Camillus. The good fathers will work you to the bone. They believe in hard labor. I understand it is one of their vows. You may be sure that you will not get much money from them."

"How do you know what their vows are?" Camillus demanded. "Would you rather beg than work?"

"Our begging is only temporary," Tiberio said pompously. "If we can last through the winter there will be plenty of fighting in the spring and places for both of us in many armies. We may even get equipment if the need of experienced men is great enough."

"I promised this Antonio Di Nicastro. At least he took my acceptance of his money as a promise."

Tiberio laughed. "You do not think that he is waiting to have you arrive? That is merely his way of getting something for his money. You are simple, Camillus. That man does not expect to see you. You go to work for the Capuchins, if there is a job there, which I doubt, and you will never see army service again."

Camillus was shaken by his friend's argument. "He did not seem the type to lie."

"He was merely making you feel better by his words or else glossing over his generosity. Many people are like that. They do not want anyone to think they are easy marks. He has already forgotten you."

"He gave me extra money. It was not like the usual gift. I think he was sincere."

"You are foolish. Come, I have given our plight a great deal of thought. I have heard that there is plenty of work at Barletta. It is not too far distant. I had quite forgotten that I have friends there, friends with money. I am certain that they will help us."

"I thought you did not want to work anywhere."

Tiberio shook his head. "Not work for a Capuchin Monastery where you will get nothing. I do not know what my friends will have us do but it will be easy compared with the monastery work and my friends will be more generous with their pay."

"Why did you not think of them before?"

"It slipped my mind. Besides we have never been in this neighborhood. Listen, Camillus, you will not regret it. If you go to this monastery do you think you can enjoy a game of cards or a little drinking? No, of course not. The fathers will have you working until you drop and never a bit of rest or play. Let us stay on our course and keep in mind the spring when we can once more follow our own work, our own lives."

"I practically promised this man."

"Have I not told you that it was no promise? He does not expect ever to see you again. If you go there you will be admitting failure to follow your own profession as a soldier."

"I do not know."

"What do you mean? You do not know what?" Tiberio cried in great exasperation. "Do you not want to rejoin the army?"

"Of course I do."

"Then let us leave at once." Tiberio stood up and Camillus, his mind still uneasy, followed.

Very pleased with his persuasion, Tiberio launched into glowing accounts of Barletta until Camillus absorbed some of his enthusiasm. However, as the journey progressed Camillus thought of Antonio Di Nicastro and he had much difficulty banishing the image. He mentioned it to Tiberio who only made fun of it, so he finally plodded along hardly hearing the words of his companion.

At midday they lunched beneath some trees and stretched out in the warm sun until the cool of the middle afternoon. Camillus felt a twinge in his leg but upon examination saw no sign to cause him concern.

"That leg worries you," Tiberio said. "I think a good part of it is your imagination. Your wound may never recur."

"I certainly hope that it does not return. It is not imagination. If you but had it you would so realize. I just felt some pain but it must be my muscles from walking."

"The road is not too good. Watch out for the holes or we will both have bad legs, broken ones. Say, here comes a wagon. They must have come through Barletta. Let us question them." They stood up and the two men in the vehicle looked at them with alarm.

"Hello, friends!" Tiberio called.

"We are but poor men going into Manfredonia to get a load of hay," one of them replied.

"Have no fear of us," Camillus reassured them. "We are not brigands, if that is what worries you. We are a couple of soldiers down on our luck and we are going to Barletta."

"Ah, Barletta."

"Is it your home town?" Tiberio asked.

"Yes, we both live there."

"Do you know the Scarpiore brothers?" Tiberio asked eagerly.

The men looked at each other. "Yes, yes, of course. Everyone knows the Scarpiore brothers."

"Do you see?" Tiberio cried with delight. "They are wealthy men, are they not, my friends?"

The two were silent.

"Come, come, speak up. Tell us about them," Tiberio demanded.

"Well, there is not much to tell. We have always been friendly with the Scarpiores. It is not us who got them into trouble."

"Trouble!" Tiberio echoed. "But they are well to do. They own a farm, a great farm."

The men shrugged. "Not now. The farm belonged to their sister whose husband died. The Scarpiore brothers are in jail."

"In jail?"

"Someone caught them stealing from the sister. Oh, it was over a long period. She had them put in jail. They, themselves, have no money. I am sorry that they are your friends."

"How long will they be in jail?"

"A long time. We must go now."

"Wait," Camillus said. "Is there much work in Barletta for those who want it?"

"There is no work. There are many idle hands. We must haul from town to town to make a living."

Camillus turned to Tiberio as the wagon moved along. "There is our luck, friend," he said bitterly.

Tiberio forced a laugh. "Do not be discouraged, Camillus.

Those two were not so bright. Come, let us move along. It will soon be night and we must hurry."

Camillus fell in alongside his friend but by now his mind was not only uneasy but his conscience bothered him. "Tiberio," he said. "You know that I am a man of my word."

"Of course. Everybody knows that. Have you not threatened many who doubted you? I have seen it myself."

"That is because I spoke the truth," Camillus said. "What do you think Antonio Di Nicastro thinks of my word?"

"Who? Oh, the man at the church door." Tiberio laughed. "Why, he does not even remember you. How could he know that Camillus de Lellis did not keep his word?"

Camillus stopped short. "Ah, that is it," he said bitterly. "He would not know, but I would. I accepted his money and promised to go to the monastery. Now, you see, our luck cannot be good for I have broken my word."

"You are a strange one, Camillus. I do not understand how you reason."

"You are wrong!" Camillus suddenly shouted in a fury. "It has bothered me since I started and now I see that there can be no good to this journey until I either retract my word or keep it. I must see Antonio Di Nicastro."

Knowing the terrible temper of his companion, Tiberio edged away. "Now, now, Camillus," he said. "Do not be hasty. I have given you counsel in this matter. Do you think I would tell you an untruth?"

"Do not quibble with me," Camillus still shouted. "I am Camillus de Lellis, even though I am a beggar. All that I had was my word and now that is gone because I listened to your devil's tongue. I should crack your head."

"Wait, wait!" Tiberio put a good distance between them. "Do not blame me for all of this."

"I cannot do that, it is true." Camillus was calmer now. "I cannot put my sins upon another. I am going back."

"Back to Manfredonia? We are almost at Barletta. You are crazy."

"I am crazy to listen to you. Will you come with me or must I go alone?"

"It is all of twelve miles. Let us go to Barletta and tomorrow we will talk about it."

"Here!" Camillus reached into his ragged shirt and tossed a hunk of bread to the grass. "That is all I have left. I am going back to explain to Signor Di Nicastro."

"Wait, wait. Listen to me," Tiberio wailed.

"I will listen to no one!" Camillus shouted and turned abruptly. Tiberio's voice still reached him and suddenly the giant swung into a loping run. At a turn in the road he glanced back. He watched while Tiberio picked up the bread from the ground, waved, and then plodded on toward Barletta. Camillus continued in the direction of Manfredonia.

Shadows lengthened and dusk settled. He passed the cart headed away from Barletta, drawn up before an inn, and continued on as night fell. One thought burned in his mind. He must explain himself to Antonio Di Nicastro.

A soft rain fell and in a short time Camillus was soaked to the skin but he did not stop. "At least I shall not have lied to him. I am sick of begging. Maybe I shall even work for a few days. That fool, Tiberio, will never work." Thoughts raced along with him, the most prominent, other than his desire to keep his word, being his hatred for the position he found himself in.

It was far into the night when he arrived in Manfredonia. "There is a light. Ah, it is a wineshop." He opened the door and entered.

A half dozen men seated about the place looked askance at the ragged, wet giant. Camillus fumbled for a coin and threw it on the counter. "Wine," he ordered and drank thirstily. Then he asked, "Do you know where the home of Signor Di Nicastro is located?"

"Signor Di Nicastro?" the wine merchant said.

"I am a stranger here but I have been asked to call upon him."

There was a laugh from the table and Camillus turned to see the amused look upon the faces of the men.

"Do you laugh at me, sir?" he said fiercely, his black eyes glinting with anger.

Sobriety immediately appeared upon their faces. "No, no, of course not; but Antonio Di Nicastro is a wealthy one."

"And I am not. Is it any business of yours?" Camillus cried in his great voice. "Tell me where I may reach him or I will not answer for your impudence."

"Wait, wait!" the wine merchant interceded. "You are very fortunate. Signor Di Nicastro lives three houses down the street on this same side."

Camillus contented himself with a baleful glance at the other customers and went again into the night. It was almost midnight when he hammered upon the front door of an imposing looking house carrying the arms and the name of the man he sought.

CHAPTER XIII

Camillus was interviewed by Father Giarro, the Guardian at the Capuchin Monastery. The genuine hospitality of the community members embarrassed the newcomer. His reaction to their all too apparent sympathy stemmed from his wounded pride and he refused as many overtures as he possibly could. He rejected the offer of clothing and he preferred to sleep in the barn rather than in the quarters shown him.

His work consisted of leading a donkey downhill, possibly a quarter mile, to a quarry and furnace where men made brick. There he loaded two great boxes one on each side of the animal which he then led back to the construction and unloaded. The donkey was stubborn and vicious and constantly tried the all too thin patience of its new master. Camillus persisted despite his almost overwhelming desire to turn and run from the place.

The very idea of going back to begging was abhorrent and the memory of it lashed at his proud spirit. In time he hoped to save enough money to re-equip himself but for the present he felt that he could bury himself in the obscurity of the monastery where it was likely none who knew him would come.

His fellow workers did not spare his pride. Even though much of what they said was intended to be good-natured banter he never accepted it as such.

"He is so tall it is hard for him to bend," one would say within his hearing.

"How is it that one so well proportioned cannot find better employment than this?" still another would say.

Camillus, almost always greatly fatigued by his labors, did not reply but the storm of anger was being stored within him. His rages were not directed at his tormentors but at himself. However, he buoyed his spirits by imaginative journeys in which he once more rode proudly with a band of marauding soldiers. He grew more silent and retreated within himself and soon the idle jesting of his fellows died away.

Toward the end of his first week he suddenly felt a terrible letdown. It was late afternoon and he was at the foot of the hill far from sight of the workmen. He threw himself behind some bushes and kicked the earth in futile rage.

"I shall never stay," he moaned, and, thinking more deeply of his lowly position, he thrust his fingers into his mouth and set his strong teeth into them until the pain restored his reason.

"I must stay. I shall stay," he determined, finally rising to his feet and resuming his miserable duties.

He went stolidly about his work, speaking as seldom as possible. His meals were served in the monastery kitchen where the brothers, like the rest of the workmen, respected his reticence and left him entirely alone.

"Feed him well, Father," the fat foreman told the Prior. "He is a great worker, the best one we have had on this job. There is no stalling or loafing, I can tell you. He certainly has surprised me."

"He is just what I thought he would be," said Father Giarro.

The foreman was puzzled. "An odd one, a very odd one. I think he has seen better days. Do you know, Father, it is very difficult for me to order him about? I just do not feel right telling him what to do."

"He has a noble bearing. Perhaps this job is what he needed to straighten himself out. Do not be too harsh and you will find that soft words will get you farther than rough ones."

The Prior worried about his new employee as the weather suddenly turned much colder and the gusts of wind grew sharper. He had noted with concern the ragged condition of Camillus' garments. "Do you not think the weather is getting colder?" he asked Camillus at the stables one morning.

"Winter is never warm, Father."

"We should like to have you sleep within the monastery. There is plenty of room and it will be more comfortable."

"I thank you, Father, but I am content."

"If you become ill you will regret your decision."

"I shall not be sick. I have roughed it for a long time. The stable is much better than I have had for some time. I am happy there."

"The cold weather will soon prevent further masonry work and we shall have to wait until the spring to resume our building," the Prior said.

Camillus felt a wave of panic. "You mean the job is closing down?"

"If the weather gets much colder they will not be able to set the brick."

"I had not thought of that." Camillus showed his concern.

"You have not been able to save much money?"

"I have saved what I could but I am not complaining, Father."

"You do feel better now that you are working? It has made you happy to a certain extent, has it not?"

"Yes, I must confess that I feel better earning my way."

"I do not want you to worry. You have been faithful. If this work is halted until the spring I should like to have you stay on here as a lay helper. We have much need of one."

"You are too good, Father," Camillus said, relief showing in his face.

"I wish that I could offer you something better. The pay will be a scudo a month along with room and board."

"That is too much."

"No, it is not enough. There is one other provision. I was in town one day last week and saw you carrying supplies back to the monastery. I also saw the children following after you and mocking at your clothes."

Camillus flushed for the scene had been a painful one. "They are only children," he said lamely. "They noticed my dagger belt and thought to have a little fun with me. I did not pay any attention to them."

Father Giarro smiled. "Ah, you are a noble man, Camillus. The only stipulation I make is that you must let Brother Antonio make you a robe from the surplus of serge cloth we have here. This is an order, Camillus. Do you accept it?"

"I have already refused Brother Antonio a number of times, but I have been foolish in my pride. I will gladly accept the clothes."

"That makes me happy."

"I do not like to accept charity."

"This is not charity. It is part of your wages."

"I will be happy to do as you say." Camillus felt his heart grow lighter with the realization that these people really liked him.

Cold weather now set in with sudden, sharp gales from the north and Camillus was glad that he had found a home. His giant figure, walking along beside the donkeys, became a familiar sight in the town of Manfredonia and many of the inhabitants greeted him cordially. He found this to his liking and was pleased at the sincerity of his new friends. He had not seen Signor Di Nicastro since the night of his flight from

Tiberio and it was a great surprise to find him at the monastery one day.

"You certainly have changed, Camillus," his benefactor told him. "Yes, you are not so hungry looking. I even discern some signs of contentment."

"At last I can thank you, sir. Yes, I am much happier."

"I have been more than repaid by the reports I have received, Camillus."

"I am pleased at that, sir."

"Yet you still wish to join the army, Camillus. Is this not so?"

"I must be honest with such a generous friend as you have been, sir. Yes, it is still my ambition to return to the military."

The other nodded. "Ah, yes. You feel that if you had money to equip yourself you would be acceptable in some army."

"I have no doubt of that."

"Well, confidence deserves confidence. You will have your chance. On the very first day in the spring when my men return to the monastery I shall come to you and ask what you most desire. I shall offer you a much better paying job but if you still wish to join the army then I shall see that you are fully equipped, including a horse and a small purse of money to keep you until you have found a place."

Camillus was overwhelmed. "This is too much, signor," he said. "You do not really know me, yet you are willing to do this."

"You are wrong. I do know you. God has been good to me so that now I have the chance to be good to someone else. I like it."

"I do not know what to say."

"Say nothing. We will see how you feel in the spring."

"That is something I shall always remember," Camillus

ST. CAMILLUS / 101

said with deep feeling. He returned to his work with renewed vigor, the promise of his patron ever present in his mind.

"You are a happy man," Brother Antonio observed that evening. A feeling of affection had developed between the brother and Camillus. They often talked over many matters.

"Is that a rarity?"

"For you, yes. You have gone about here like a pillar of storm and now you are pure sunshine."

"I am happy that I will be able to rejoin the army in the spring."

"You have come into some money?"

"No, but I have a promise."

"The only promise that is good is God's," the brother said.

"Signor Di Nicastro's promise is good enough for me."

The religious looked at him with searching eyes. "You do not know yourself, Camillus," he said slowly. "Remember what I have said to you. Only the promise of God is good."

"Do you mean that the word of Signor Di Nicastro is not good?" Camillus was annoyed.

"I did not say that. Signor Di Nicastro is an excellent man. Do you stop to think that his promise, whatever it might be, may never be fulfilled? You do not even know that his promise is good. You may not be happy with it. We only know the promise of God is good, that it always will be."

"Brother Antonio is an odd one," Camillus muttered as he went about his way. "I have no quarrel with God. He made it almost sound that way. We all know that the promise of God is good. Certainly the word of a man like Signor Di Nicastro is good, also."

The remarks of the brother often returned to his mind and caused him unrest. They also turned his mind more toward God.

Father Giarro came to him a week later. "I have a special journey for you to make, Camillus. You are to go with the two donkeys to the Capuchins at St. John Rotondo Monastery. You will have to stay there overnight."

Camillus was delighted at the prospect of a change.

"They have a surplus of wine, I know," Father Giarro said. "But you will tell the Guardian that we have brought him some wine that we know he must need and in exchange would like some flour. We would like five bags, if his Christian soul can be so charitable."

"But you have already said that they have a surplus of wine?"

"Of course, of course, but we have little flour. It is the same trick he has played on us many times. The good fathers at St. John Rotondo cannot complain of too much wine but we can complain of too little flour."

"I shall be happy to go, Father."

"Be ready in the morning."

Camillus accordingly set out on his trip with a gay heart. The promise of Signor Di Nicastro had cast a spell about him that lifted his previous despondency.

The road to St. John Rotondo Monastery was a rough one, in need of much repairs, but to Camillus it was like a bed of velvet. Memories of the past flooded over him and in the future he saw himself riding at the head of a brave band of adventurers. The journey passed quickly and he was greeted heartily at the gates of the monastery.

"I know your errand," the Guardian said with a quiet smile. "You are loaded with wine for us and so too are our cellars."

Camillus was dismayed at the direct statement. "We have so little flour, Father," he stammered.

The other smiled. "Do not say anything. My old friend,

Father Giarro, is a smart man. If he has little flour we shall add to it, regardless of the wine. Come in, my son, rest for the night. In the morning you shall have eight bags instead of five. We will overwhelm your good superior with our generosity."

"But I am not of the congregation, Father."

"Your clothes tell me that you are not one of the professed but you are still one of us. Oh, yes, I can see that quite clearly."

Camillus was greatly pleased at the warmth and hospitality of his reception and especially the words of the superior. "You are most kind to me, Father," he said. Never before had he been so happy as he followed one of the brothers to the cell allotted him.

Camillus stared out of the little window. It was late afternoon and the winter sun, not warm, slanted across the bare fields and bathed the old monastery in a soft glow. The low murmur of voices in the orderly recital of a litany reached his ears. The cadence of the prayer was like a soothing balm. Strife and contest were limitless miles away and all was peace. For the first time in many years the tumultuous nature of Camillus de Lellis rested in the calm haven of complete tranquillity.

CHAPTER XIV

Camillus tightened the donkeys' belts and was about to start when a gentle hand touched his arm.

"Good morning, Father." He faced the Guardian.

"I almost missed you," the priest said. "I saw you at Mass this morning and thought I should personally bid you farewell."

"You have been very kind, Father. My visit here has been a happy one, indeed."

"It is only that you have had a few hours to rest and think, Camillus. You have always found a warm reception in the houses of the Lord. Is this not so?"

"You are right, Father. I have always been made to feel welcome. You think of others and not of yourselves, but I am always thinking of my own troubles and there is no room for anything else."

The Guardian laughed. "Oh, we think of ourselves, too. That possibly is why we have entered religion, thinking first of saving our own souls. But in order to do that we must also think of others, especially when we consider the golden rule."

He paused for a moment and then spoke again. "Your life has not been an easy one."

"Oh, I would not say that, Father. Anyway, it has been of my own making. I have no one to blame but myself."

"That is an excellent confession, son. Most people blame their lives on someone or something else. When I speak of an uneasy life I do not mean the physical or financial life. I mean the moral life. You see, Camillus, each man leads a variety of lives but most are interested in only the one that most directly affects him. Sad to say, this is usually not the moral one. The only time we priests are certain that grave attention will be given to the moral is when a man stops to think of the enormous gain and loss associated with it, usually at the time of his death."

Camillus was uneasy. "Well, Father, I am one of those who have spent most of their time with the physical and, yes, the financial life, for they go hand in hand. However, I have not willingly hurt any man."

"Only yourself," the priest said gently. "Remember, also, my son, it is for yourself alone that you will be held accountable."

"Why do you talk to me like this, Father?" Camillus asked in sudden confusion.

"Because in a short time you have become dear to me. I can feel your restless spirit. It was here when you arrived last night and once more, now that you are leaving, I can feel it coming back. On your return trip think over your life as a soldier and a wanderer. Ask yourself the question: what has my life gained for me so far?"

"Gained for me?"

"Oh, not in the material sense. What has it gained you in peace of mind?"

Camillus stared at the priest.

"It is only that you have never given yourself time to think. There will be nothing to bother you for the next few hours. Think of Camillus de Lellis, not as a soldier but as a child of God. Go now and think kindly of an old man who only wishes your happiness. Go with God's blessing."

"Thank you, Father," Camillus said humbly. He was deeply

affected by the old man's words, though a little confused.

The day was beautifully clear, crisp and cold. The hard canopy of blue sky was unmarred by even one cloud and the distant sun sent flashing lights from the thousands of ice pebbles that sparkled in the trees.

Camillus walked beside the donkeys, heedless of the hard packed, rutted road, for his mind could not shake off the final words of the Guardian. He tried to brush aside the picture the old man had painted but it persisted.

The panorama of his own life unfolded in a series of disquieting scenes. Almost always he saw himself as vain, proud, tempestuous, willful.

"I must get away from these fathers or they will drive me mad," he said aloud, knowing that his only hours of peace had been in their company.

The little procession moved along the road and Camillus did not even see those infrequent fellow travelers who passed and waved. "I cannot stand much more of my mixed up affairs. If I but stay with them until spring Signor Di Nicastro will then rescue me."

"Rescue me? From what? From their friendship and their solicitude? No one else has ever even thought of where I am going. Then again, neither have I. Where am I going? Am I going to a lonely deathbed like my father? I will not have even a child to mourn me. He had one, but what a child. I do not deserve to even mourn for him. I should mourn for myself. I do not know where I am going."

He trudged on and suddenly cried out. "If only I had never talked to him. Ah, if only I had some wine. It would clear my head of all this buzzing. That is what I need."

He searched his pockets but could not find a single coin. The tiny hoard that he had managed to save was back at the monastery. He tore open the package of refreshments that had been put up for him by the brothers. There was a bottle but it contained only water. In a sudden rage he hurled it against a rock.

Immediately he was sorry. "The good Father is right. I think only of the physical," he cried. Then he saw a little inn not fifty yards distant. "Physical or not," he declared, "there is a wineshop and I have no intention of passing it by. I shall have a drink." He beat his switch against the sides of the pack animals who completely ignored him and continued their steady way.

Reaching the building he tied the donkeys to a hitching post. "He surely will give me credit for a drink. I need it as I never have before. I am beset by the devil's own pictures. I do not know whether I am coming or going. Yes, a drink will surely steady me. If he does not give me credit I will give him the credit of this switch."

He entered with his old truculence and swagger. As he stepped into the doorway he came face to face with a tall, black-robed priest. The calm eyes of the cleric, in a strange white face, unnerved the giant for a moment. He stepped to one side to allow the priest to pass.

"You are in great haste, my son." The voice was calm and arresting.

"They are everywhere, bothering me," Camillus thought desperately. "I have had a long journey. I am thirsty," he said, not too graciously.

"The wine is excellent here."

"That is good, thank you." Camillus watched the priest go down the road, then made his way to the bar.

"Good day, signor." The innkeeper was a short, fat man with an ingratiating smile.

"Good day to you. Give me a bottle of your best wine, cooled, I hope."

"Ah, you are a discerning man." The shopkeeper produced a bottle that glistened in the dim light. "My wine is cooled by my own spring. See, I have an outlet here, under the counter." The man was talkative but Camillus did not return his loquacity. He snatched the bottle and with trembling hands lifted it to his lips and drank with great swallows.

"That is not the way to drink my wine," the man cried. "Slowly, slowly, so that you may taste it."

Camillus wiped some drops from his chin. "Silence!" he shouted. "I am drinking this wine my own way. Bring me another at once." He returned to the bottle and a shadow from the doorway fell across the counter.

Camillus started when he saw that the priest had returned and was now sitting on a bench inside the door. He stared at the cleric but apparently the man was not looking at him. Camillus turned to receive the bottle from the innkeeper.

The owner appeared nervous as he appraised the giant. "You will pay now, signor. It is my custom after the first bottle."

Camillus drained the bottle and grasped his hand about the second one. He stared at the speaker. "You will get your money, you oaf," he shouted. "Do you think I am a thief?"

"It is not that, signor. It is the custom."

"Then keep your tongue quiet. I will drink all the wine I want and pay for it when I will."

A look of horror flashed across the fat face of the owner and without another word he turned and ran through the back door.

Camillus returned to the bottle, his rage somewhat subdued. The wine was good and it refreshed him so that his mind was clearer.

"I hope you have the money to pay for that drink," a quiet voice reached him and he turned to see the priest.

"Do I look like a thief?" he cried.

"I know you are not a thief." The smile disarmed Camillus. "However, you do look like a thirsty man with no money to pay for that expensive wine."

Camillus trembled and a sense of uneasiness seized him. "What is it to you?" he said. He was sorry immediately for his rudeness.

"Nothing, my son, nothing that you would understand. It will, however, be something to you and very shortly."

"What do you mean?"

"You do not know our innkeeper. He is not too hospitable. Look down the road."

Camillus went to the window. The proprietor, waving his hands and talking excitedly, was returning, flanked by two uniformed men listening attentively.

"The devil, the swine!" Camillus snatched up the heavy, wooden bar used to bolt the door.

"Wait, my friend." The priest walked over to the counter and put a handful of silver coins on top of it. "This is a much easier way."

"I do not want your money," Camillus exclaimed to hide his sudden shame.

"No, but the innkeeper does," the other returned dryly.

Camillus felt a rush of remorse. "On my word I do not do this sort of thing regularly," he said. "It is only that I am very much troubled this day. Father, I am grateful for your loan. I will be by here in a few days. I have money and I will bring it and repay you. Whom shall I ask for?"

"There is no need to ask for anyone. Pretend it is yours, for surely it is. I will enjoy seeing Gaetano's face when he realizes that you are a man of means. It may also teach him a much overdue lesson." He went back to the bench, opened a prayer book, and became absorbed.

"There he is! There he is, still drinking my wine!" the innkeeper shouted as he came through the door.

"Who are you?" one of the officers demanded of Camillus as they ranged alongside.

"I am no one to give an account to you," Camillus said rudely. "What is that madman shouting about?"

"He declares you have taken his wine and have refused to pay for it. We are the police. Answer to this charge."

"What do you call that?" Camillus pointed to the scattered coin. "I said I would pay when I was ready. I did not refuse to pay. He is a mad one, I tell you. Well, count the money. There is enough and more."

"So!" The policeman doing the talking turned on Gaetano in a most unfriendly manner. "You are too fast with your tongue, Gaetano. It is you we should arrest for breach of the peace and for falsely accusing this man."

"I do not understand," the innkeeper protested.

"Wait," Camillus said. "Give these good men a bottle to take back with them. I will pay."

"You are most kind." The officer gratefully took the proffered wine and with threatening words and glances at the owner left the place.

"I am sorry, signor. I was too hasty."

"No more talk from you," Camillus said fiercely, then looked over at the bench. "Where is the priest?"

"The priest? The priest?" The man was suddenly terrified at the wild look in the other's eyes.

"Yes, you stupid. I said the priest. Where is the priest who was leaving here as I entered? He came back and sat on the bench."

"There was no priest here, signor. I have seen no priest inside these walls since Tomaso Rasso was suddenly taken ill a year ago."

"Shut your mouth!" Camillus ran to the door and strained his eyes in all directions. "Where can he have gone to?"

"The heat is bad this morning, signor." The owner was now completely terrified. "Listen, my good friend. Sit down and I will make a present to you of my finest bottle."

"I do not want your stinking wine!" Camillus shouted. "I want to see the priest." He ran out of the building but there was no one to be seen. Only the donkeys stood patiently waiting.

He returned to the inn and accosted the trembling owner. "Did you not see the priest here but a short time ago?" His tones, now calm, did not appease the man.

"I swear that I have seen no priest. The nearest one is five miles away, an old man who cannot walk too well. Listen, signor, the day is a hot one. The heat has affected you. Perhaps if you rested and had a bottle?"

"You fool. It is the month of February and cold. Do not act as if I were insane." He suddenly turned and ran from the place. He went around the building and still there was no sign. "I am going mad," he exclaimed. "I did not imagine this thing." He hastily untied the donkeys and set off down the road. Glancing back he saw the innkeeper hurriedly putting up his shutters. While he watched, the man went in and slammed the door.

The weather changed and rain began to fall but Camillus did not feel it soak into his clothes or beat against his face.

He was suddenly most calm and a strange quickening of his pulse took place. "I do not understand it," he said aloud. "At last the world is growing peaceful."

He came to the top of a hill and saw in the distance the gray walls of the monastery toward which he was headed. "Home," he said. "Yes, that is my home. There is no trouble there for me. There is only peace."

For a long time he looked across the valley then suddenly threw himself to the ground striking with his clenched fist at the hard earth. He cried aloud in a strange, choking voice and finally, exhausted, buried his face.

Eventually he looked up at the heavens. He felt strangely alone in the entire place but there was also the feeling of a new contentment, a new reasoning.

"Lord, have pity on me, a miserable sinner. Unhappy am I that I have not known Thee sooner. Grant me time to do penance, to love Thee. Pardon, oh Lord, this great sinner. I cannot fight more except for Thee."

The day was February 2, 1575, the Feast of the Purification of the Blessed Virgin.

CHAPTER XV

The next morning Camillus presented himself to the Director.

"Sit down, Camillus. I would like to hear what news you gathered at St. John Rotondo. I noticed that you brought back more than we asked."

"They were very generous, Father. But it is not of my journey that I would like to talk, if you can spare me a few minutes."

"I have all the time in the world to listen to what you have to say, Camillus. Make yourself comfortable. You are sitting on the edge of that chair as if nails were in the seat of it."

"What I have to say may sound strange and I suppose bold, but I have a request to make, Father."

"If it is possible, consider it granted."

"I want to stay here. I want to join the Capuchins and give my life to the Lord." Camillus pleaded with great passion.

A look of genuine pleasure came across the face of the priest. "I have prayed for this," he said, to the other's astonishment. "I have long felt that your way of life was different from what it ought to be. Have you considered this well, Camillus?"

"I lay awake all of last night and have thought it out well. Many times in my past life I have had the urge but this is an overpowering one that I feel I must not pass by. I know that it is the only road to my happiness."

"You will be welcome. I shall have to receive the authority

of my superior. Believe me, I shall plead for you. If you are accepted, and I have no doubt you will be, you will have to go to Trivento for your novitiate studies. Kneel and I will bless you and ask for God's help."

Camillus now underwent the experience of all reformed men. Suspicion and incredulity were his lot. Despite the attempt of some of the brothers to disguise their feelings they were all too perceptible. Strangely, he did not mind. He went his way on assigned duties with an ardor that stunned his fellows. His silent bitterness and aloof hostility disappeared and there was no task he would not do if but a hint were dropped.

The Guardian had assigned him to the kitchen where the work was most difficult and where he did an excellent job. As soon as he completed his work he usually sought the outside where the weather was now rigorous and insisted on sharing the chores. A few weeks elapsed and then came the approval of the Superior to allow Camillus to study within the order.

There was great rejoicing in the monastery and it was with a glad yet sad heart that Camillus one morning said good-by and set out on foot for Trivento, a good distance, to begin his novitiate. The world was at last calm for Camillus de Lellis and he knew that he had never been happier. Even the wound on his ankle and foot seemed to have completely healed although a slight redness marked the affected spot.

His arrival at Trivento was a quiet one for it was an everyday event to receive recruits. Here in pleasant surroundings Camillus was to try to make good. He prayed long and earnestly.

Such was his fervor and humility that he was referred to with affection as the Humble Brother. He was the first to answer the call of duty, most exacting in the smallest rule, self-sacrificing in his work, and the last one to retire each night.

The Guardian and the brothers, alarmed at his display of intense and most unusual energy, were forced to warn him and insist upon a lessening of his labors. Within a few months Camillus had become most popular.

Now there was visited upon him the first of that long list of trials that might have broken the will of a less determined man. The reappearance of the wound took place. It became worse this time than it had ever been, spreading rapidly over foot, ankle, and leg. He could hardly stand and, to add to his discomfort and embarrassment, a nauseous odor emanated from the sores.

Camillus knelt many nights in prayer in his barren cell, but his handicap grew increasingly worse. Finally, in desperation he sought out the Director. Immediately he was ordered to the infirmary where an examination took place.

The old monk in charge shook his head. "It is very bad. I do not know what to call it." He turned to the Director who was anxiously listening. "It needs treatment that I cannot give."

"Have you no idea what it is?"

"It could be called an ulcer yet it is different. I do not understand the history of this wound as Camillus has recounted it. It comes and goes and I cannot even attempt to say why."

"Camillus has told me that a cure was effected at St. Giacomo Hospital in Rome," the Director said.

"They naturally would be able to do better than we could," the infirmarian replied. "I would suggest that he go there for treatment. If they have been successful once they well may be again."

Camillus was uneasy. "I am afraid, Father, that the authorities at St. Giacomo would never allow me to return." He hung his head. "My record there, may God forgive me, was certainly not of the best."

"Do not let that bother you." The superior placed his hand on the patient's shoulder. "Tomorrow you will go to Rome. I shall give you a letter telling of your devotion here. Do not be alarmed. You will be admitted."

Camillus wept openly. "Does this mean that I cannot become a Capuchin?" he cried. "I suppose it does. God could not want such a wretch as I am in His service."

"Here, you must not talk like that," the Director said sternly. "God is infinite in His mercy. I daresay many worse than you have been received back in His arms. You will be welcome here as soon as the wounds heal. We want you. You would be a distinct addition to our community.

"You are most kind to me, Father."

"Only sensible. It is God you must always thank. This is just another trial He has given you. You will overcome it. You will be cured and you will return here. Be of much faith and strong heart."

And so it came about that Camillus de Lellis once more presented himself at the Hospital of St. Giacomo in Rome. It was only through the intercession of the superior at Trivento that he was allowed entrance into the institution. The authorities were reluctant at first, but they changed their minds.

The sick in St. Giacomo got no more attention than they had previously. In fact, they were so neglected that it was just short of a public scandal. Camillus spent most of his time at the bedside of the ill and sought little rest for himself. This experience made him aware of the awful conditions inside the hospital. The ones in charge still found it difficult to secure proper employees. They were forced to take on almost anyone who applied for work.

Patients, in the absence of proper supervision, were left without food or even drink. Certain high fever cases were known to drink oil from lamps or even worse in desperation. Their beds remained untouched, however weak the sick were, and so they rotted in their own filth. Some, attempting to help themselves, fell out of bed and died on the floor and the brutal attendants ignored them. Almost alone in his tremendous task, Camillus encountered animosity at many turns from his fellow workers. They accused him of trying to attract the attention of the authorities to their neglect.

One lonely night, as was his custom, Camillus rose from his bed, knelt for a short prayer, and set out for the ward assigned him. The corridors were long and only sparsely lighted by flickering lamps. It was early spring and cold. Camillus shivered as he made his way across the floors, his lips moving in prayer for those whose groans reached him. At the door of his ward he heard loud cries and he hurried forward, only to stop aghast at the sight before his eyes.

In the middle of the aisle a half naked patient, attired in the short jumper of the hospital, lay writhing on the floor under the blows of a stick wielded by the night attendant, a burly, black bearded man named Francisco Rocchi. The other patients, cowering and half slumped on their pallets, watched in mute terror.

"You stop your yelling!" Rocchi cried, kicking at the prostrate figure.

A rage he had not known for months seized Camillus and he covered the distance of yards with great bounds, snatching the club from the snarling employee. Rocchi started back from the infuriated face.

"What are you doing?" Camillus shouted.

"I cannot stand this one," the other said sullenly. "I am no sooner seated than he moans and calls for something, water, food, anything to bother me."

Camillus dropped the stick and carried the moaning victim to his bed where he gently bathed him, speaking in soft tones all the time. He covered the man, brought him water, and gave him whatever other assistance he could.

Rocchi watched the proceedings and finally went over and stood by the bed. "You are spoiling these pigs," he said. "You give them too much attention during the day so that we at night must follow your example. The stick is still the best for them."

Camillus continued to sooth the patient until in a few minutes he fell into an exhausted sleep. Then he turned to Rocchi. "Come, Francisco, I will explain something to you," he said quietly, although his blood raced madly.

"Explain to me? You are a fool, De Lellis."

"Perhaps, but come with me." Camillus motioned with his hand and they walked past the long line of fearful staring eyes. Camillus quietly closed the big doors and they were alone in the corridor.

"You may have badly hurt that patient," he said. "You must always remember that these are Christ's sick."

"What?" Rocchi was astounded.

"These sick people are the sick of Christ."

The look of incredulity was followed by a contemptuous leer. "Then let Christ take care of them."

This brutal remark unleashed the anger that Camillus had tried to keep in check. He held the burly attendant with one hand and swung madly with the other, raining powerful blows at Rocchi's face. It was impossible to break the hold that Camillus had upon him and in a few minutes the man's face was reduced to a bloody mess. Finally, Camillus sent him tumbling to the floor where he desperately tried to sit up, then fell back groaning.

"Now listen!" Camillus said with bared teeth. "If you ever touch a patient other than with gentleness, you shall answer to me."

"You are a madman," Rocchi gasped, finally sitting up. His eyes widened as he looked beyond Camillus. "Ah, you will get yours now. Father, Father, this man is insane. He has almost killed me."

Camillus turned to meet one of the directors. At his side was Philip Neri, a priest who had often stopped in the halls to talk to De Lellis.

"What does this mean?" the director asked. "Fighting in the hospital. You will answer for this at once."

"He has no business in the ward at night," Rocchi cried, staggering to his feet. "He came in and dragged me out into the corridor to assault me."

Camillus noticed that the face of Philip Neri had no sign of anger upon it. He was calm and Camillus suddenly knew that he had a friend who would believe him.

"What have you to say, De Lellis?" the priest asked quietly.

"I found this man beating and kicking a patient he had dragged from the bed and thrown to the floor."

Camillus saw that Philip Neri had now been touched. His eyes blazed at the muttering Rocchi. "What have you to say?"

"Kicking a patient?" the director echoed.

"This man, De Lellis, is a devil," Rocchi cried. "He has no right to come here at night. He is always snooping around."

"Wait!" Philip went into the ward and there was a momentary silence. He returned almost immediately and looked hard at the fumbling Rocchi. "De Lellis has told the truth," he declared. "How could anyone act so brutally as this

Rocchi? Poor man that you are, God will demand an answer for this night's work."

"He had it coming to him," Rocchi replied sullenly. "This De Lellis has disorganized the hospital with his attentions to those beggars. He is trying to make a fool of all the other attendants."

"I will make more than that of you," Camillus threatened and the other backed away.

"Get out of here!" the director told the wretched man. "Get out of this hospital at once or I will have you arrested. Never let me see you here again."

Rocchi started to whine but, as Camillus moved toward him, he took off down the long corridor.

"This is a terrible thing," the director said. "I do not approve of fighting in the hospital, but in this instance, De Lellis, I do not blame you. The man needed such punishment. He would not understand any other kind. Tomorrow morning, please report to my office. Oh, it is not for discipline. I have something better in mind."

"If you have time please come to my place, too," Philip Neri said, affectionately tapping Camillus on the shoulder.

De Lellis watched them out of sight, then suddenly knelt on the stone floor and clasped his hands in prayer.

"Oh Lord, forgive my anger. Forgive me for what I have done. I thought that I was master of myself, but I am not yet. Help me to overcome this evil temper. Make me worthy of Thy service, oh Lord."

CHAPTER XVI

Camillus de Lellis was made infirmarian, overseer of a group of workers in certain wards. This did not mitigate any of his efforts, for his whole creed was contained in a simple statement made during a conversation with Philip Neri. "I am doing this for Christ," Camillus said. "I see him in the sick and what poor efforts I make are directed toward pleasing Him."

"There is no higher motive in life. In your new position as infirmarian you will be afforded a much larger field in which to work."

"I am afraid that I will not prove worthy."

"You alone are in doubt. Everyone else is certain of your success."

Within a matter of days those servants assigned to Camillus found that so long as the patients were not neglected they got along surprisingly well with their new supervisor, even to the extent of having his valuable physical assistance. Camillus spent most of his time within the walls of the hospital. The brief moments of freedom he allowed himself he spent wandering in the streets of Rome, invariably ending in the extremely poor sections.

His salary increase, though small, gave him the chance to be more generous with those he met. All of his extra money was spent in acts of kindness toward the poor and the sick. Whenever he returned from his walks he was penniless but he had left behind grateful if somewhat astonished children and beggars, sudden recipients of bread, sweetmeats, or a bit of money.

After seven months as infirmarian he was again called before the Board of Directors. The Maestro De Casa sat at the head of a table around which were grouped the four Guardians who carried out his orders. The hospital was so large that it required these assistants, each with one section of the institution under his care.

The Maestro came directly to the point. "You, of course, know that we have an office called that of Guardaroba. This position entails the greatest responsibility. It carried the full supervision of all the material effects of the hospital. It deals not only with the help but also with making requisitions for supplies and the purchase of many articles. You know this?"

"I know some of the work of that office." Camillus was puzzled. "I have been too busy to acquaint myself with all the duties, but it is apparent there is tremendous responsibility attached to it."

"There is a vacancy in the office and we want you to have it."

"You mean you wish me to take the job of Guardaroba?"

"That is just it."

"But I am not worthy. Pray, let me but work for another. The position is too high for the likes of me."

"We are of a different mind, Camillus. Your duties will start this day. Pick up your effects and bring them here. We will give you full instructions in your new office. God will assist you for you are a good and honorable man."

Tears welled up in Camillus' eyes. "Pardon me, Signors. It is only that you have called me an honorable man. I am happy for that."

The position proved to be all that the authorities had declared. Camillus still found time to visit the wards and he made this his daily practice, but the many hours he spent sitting at a desk seemed beneficial to his leg which was soon almost completely healed.

One thing happened in the routine of his new duties that had far-reaching physical effects. In fact the results of the incident remained with Camillus his entire lifetime. On a cold, winter day he descended to the kitchen early in the morning to supervise the receipt of a large shipment of flour. Camillus had introduced a system of spot checking all purchases that came into the hospital and the results had been a marked increase in the inventory of goods on hand. Some of the older kitchen help resented this and made it apparent. Camillus quickly put them in their proper places and his method was continued.

He arrived this certain day just as the last of the shipments of flour had been placed in the storehouse. The dealer and two hospital aides were looking over some sheets of paper.

"You are early today." Camillus spoke pleasantly to the merchant.

"Yes, Signor Guardaroba, we are very busy, so we thought we would come to the hospital on the first delivery." The dealer was a short, powerfully built man with swarthy features and a ready smile.

"An excellent idea. May I have the invoice, please?"

"It has already been checked, signor. It is only flour this morning, thirty-two bags."

"Thirty-two bags?"

"Yes, everything is fine. We will call later in the day with the other supplies."

"But the invoice, signor. May I have it?" Camillus put forth his hand and was reluctantly handed the paper.

He carefully scanned the figures. "The price never seems to go down," he remarked.

"It is the cheapest price I can give. You insist on a better quality than we used to deliver. Will you please sign it and we shall get on our way."

"I would rather pay a higher price for good quality. Well, we shall see." He started for the storeroom.

"It is already checked, signor," the dealer said.

"Yes, I heard you say that," Camillus replied. "It is only that sometimes I like to check things myself."

"One of your men, Rocco, has already done that," the dealer said. "This will be a great delay for me and do away with all the advantages of our early start."

"Such a bill is well worth it." Camillus called to one of the help and asked for a count.

"I signed in thirty-two bags, Guardaroba."

Camillus opened the door and one glance convinced him that something was not right. "Count them," he ordered.

"But I already have." This time Rocco spoke up, suddenly frightened.

"Then I will count them myself." Camillus felt his anger rising. "I will personally move them to the other side of the bin. Count with me."

Apparently exerting little effort he lifted and tossed each bag separately into another bin and called out the number. Rocco repeated in a stuttering tone.

"Twenty-two." It was the final figure. Turning, Camillus found that half the kitchen force was ringed around the door, attracted by the sound of loud voices.

"Twenty-two!" he shouted in his thunderous tones, fixing a terrible glare upon the dealer and Rocco.

"There, there must be a mistake. How could it have happened?" The dealer was the first to recover and he made a bold effort to save the situation.

"There is a mistake, the mistake of a thief!" Camillus

shouted. "You are not only a thief yourself but you have made thieves of my help with your petty, filthy money."

"You cannot talk to me like this. I am a respectable merchant. Do not forget that I have many friends who are in authority in this place. I will not stand this abuse."

The dealer knew that his only recourse was in a bold front, but he had selected the wrong approach to Camillus. Uttering a great roar that sent his help scattering, Camillus seized the stocky dealer and lifted him high above his head. "I shall beat your thieving head against the wall," he shouted, marching from the storeroom to the huge kitchen, the victim screaming in fear and futilely attempting to get loose.

It was Rocco who delayed the threatened punishment by quite unwittingly racing madly from the scene, emitting frightened yells as he disappeared through the door.

Camillus saw him and like a veil his anger dropped away. He put the man down with a thud and stood staring after Rocco, whose face showed how completely terrified he was. "I have done it again," Camillus thought.

The others hastily retreated from the kitchen and the dealer scrambled up from the floor and ran after his accomplice.

"My temper is as bad as ever," Camillus thought. "Ah, surely God will punish me for such an outburst of anger." Without further words he left and retired with lagging steps to his room where he knelt beside his bed and prayed a long time. Suddenly a sharp, wrenching pain shot through his groin and stomach and he cried out in agony. He barely managed to drag himself erect and fall across the bed. Sometime later, his absence noted, an attendant found him convulsed with agony.

That night, propped up in bed, Camillus received a visit from Philip Neri. "So you, too, are a sick man." The priest smiled. "I heard about your trouble and came personally to comfort the great comforter."

"I am glad we are alone, Father," Camillus said. "This is a just punishment from our Lord for my terrible temper and the sin of anger."

Philip smiled again as he sat down. "I hate to disappoint you, Camillus. In all fairness I do not think we can blame the Lord for your ailment. He did not tell you to swing a two hundred pound thief over your head. Oh, yes, I heard the story. You have simply ruptured yourself."

"I deserve it."

"Yours was a just anger, although I think you carried it a little too far after tossing twenty-two hundred pounds of flour about. You have finally learned that physical violence does not settle a problem."

"A wicked, wicked temper," Camillus muttered.

"Woe to the flour dealer and his companions." Philip now grew solemn. "You have a bad rupture, Camillus. It is certainly going to hinder you for some time. I have been told that you will have to wear a heavy iron truss, perhaps for years."

"I shall do without it for penance."

"And die in agony. No, you must do as the doctors tell you. If you insist that this is punishment it will be a constant reminder to approach your problems more quietly."

Philip was right. Camillus would wear the truss for years. He was to suffer from the incident the rest of his days. The additional pain, however, did not deter the Guardaroba from fulfilling his duties with a care and exactness that earned high praise. His initial ailment, the mysterious ulcerous condition of his leg, was now a source of satisfaction; not a sign of it remained.

At this time he decided to try again to join the Capuchins.

Despite the objections of the hospital authorities he carried through his resolve and returned to the monastery where he was received with great rejoicing. He entered into his old duties with a new zest and when he had accomplished his labors he spent long hours before the Blessed Sacrament praying for the sick whose memory haunted him. He was sent to Tagliacozzo Novitiate in the Abruzzi District.

Shortly after this the blow came. The sore on his leg suddenly reappeared with an increased virulence. As a result the Capuchins had no other option than to send him away for the second and last time. Once again Camillus de Lellis faced a great decision.

CHAPTER XVII

Camillus returned to St. Giacomo in a most distressed mental state but his welcome from both the authorities and the patients was so overwhelming that he felt his zest for living return at once.

He confided in Philip Neri. "I intend to do something worthwhile here. I should like to change the attitude of the servants. They do not seem to have any real interest or sympathy toward the patients."

"You are right. It is a thankless job from a money viewpoint, and that is what seems to govern most people. Only when one looks to God will he get his reward for such work. The type we are forced to hire never think of such a thing. You know the tremendous turnover in employees in this place. You might say we have only vagrant workers. We cannot afford higher pay so we must be content with these."

"There is one way," Camillus said thoughtfully.

"And that?"

"A special religious society should be created for the care of the sick, to serve them without pay and only for the love of Christ."

Philip looked at him sharply. "There are enough orders in the Church already," he replied. "It would be most difficult to get any authority to do this thing. Incidentally, Camillus, there is a special honor coming to you and it is my pleasure to announce it. You have an excellent reputation and that is why you are to be promoted."

"Promoted? But I have just returned and am deeply grateful that even my old position was still open to me."

"There was little doubt that you would return. Even if your leg had not caused you trouble I am of the opinion that you could not have lived happily without your sick."

"They were constantly on my mind," Camillus confessed.

"They have become a part of you."

"But what is this talk of a promotion, Father?"

"The matter has been given great thought and it is the unanimous desire of the entire hospital board that you be the new Maestro De Casa."

"Maestro De Casa?" Camillus was so amazed that he stood up. "No, Father, that cannot be. It is impossible."

"Sit down, Camillus," Philip said firmly.

"I cannot believe this." Camillus sat down, stunned.

"You are now a man of stature. You are to be the General Superintendent of St. Giacomo. You have already proved yourself. Now, my friend, let us see that you do your best to reform the servant situation. You will have every opportunity to bring your ideas into action."

Camillus went at once to the chapel where he spent long hours in prayer. He could hardly believe the tremendous news, yet within a week he found himself settled in the most authoritative position at the hospital. There was not enough time for him to do the work he desired and he often went whole days with but a few hours sleep, yet his remarkable constitution carried him through the hard routine.

Camillus gave most of the credit for accomplishment to two exceptional helpers. "I am not alone in this work," he said to Philip Neri. "God has sent me some excellent helpers. They are not many but each is worth a dozen of the ordinary. You know the most excellent Curzio Lodi. In fact I have been told you sent him here."

"It was my privilege. He is the one from Aquilla. A most outstanding man, Camillus."

"I think he is a saint. Then there is another, my new Guardaroba, Bernadino Norcino."

Philip smiled. "The three of you are excellent models, my friend."

It was during a stormy night that one of the doctors came upon the Maestro De Casa and Bernadino Norcino sitting for a brief rest in one of the small rooms adjoining a ward. "I have been looking for you, Maestro," the physician said. "We have just had a consultation in the surgery about a patient who was admitted this evening. He has a broken leg, highly infected and gangrenous. We have decided upon amputation and the instruments are already beneath the patient's bed for an early morning operation. We cannot lose any more time. We have given him opiates but as you know they are not too effective. He is in pain and restless. He is a former soldier and I think your presence would help him."

"Please take me to him at once." Camillus was already at the door.

"Will you call me if you need rest?" Bernadino asked. "In fact, why do we not take turns during the night watch?"

"You are most kind," Camillus replied. "This man, however, was a soldier and I think he would be better with an old relic of the wars such as I. If I do need you, though, I certainly will call."

Camillus went down the hall with the physician to where a tiny lamp illuminated the room set aside for surgery. Only one of a dozen beds was occupied and that by a muttering, restless man. Camillus approached the sufferer. He noted with practiced eye that the patient had been securely tied to the pallet. Bending over the haggard face he stared into the pain-filled eyes. Memories crashed into his mind and he found himself trembling. "Good Lord, this cannot be my old friend," he breathed, "Albrecht, Albrecht Horzen."

"Who calls my name? Oh, God, answer me." The words were very ragged.

"It is I, Camillus de Lellis."

"Camillus? Camillus de Lellis. But where am I? I am dead and in hell."

"Not yet, fortunately for both of us." Camillus took a cloth and wet it and tenderly bathed the patient's brow.

"Camillus de Lellis. I loved that man. He was with me that day, many days. Where am I? I am going mad with pain."

"You are in the hospital and we are going to help you, Albrecht. Yes, it is your old friend, Camillus, and I work here helping to care for the sick. I am here to help you."

"Camillus in a hospital? I am in the hospital? I remember, now. It is you, I can see. You always told the truth. Yes, it is you, Camillus de Lellis. No one else was so big. What madness is this?"

"It is no madness, Albrecht." Camillus continued his bathing. "I am here as a worker."

"Ah, your leg. How you worried about it. But you still have it, Camillus." His voice rose to a cry of fear. "I'm going to lose my leg! You still have yours that you worried so much about, and tomorrow they will take mine."

The patient screamed in his terror and the heart of Camillus contracted. "Perhaps they will save it, my friend."

"Do not perhaps me, Camillus. It is not like you. I have heard them. Oh, God, why not a cannon ball or a sword in the years past? Help me, Camillus. Help me. I am afraid." The sweat oozed from his forehead.

"You must be quiet, Albrecht. Here, I will give you this to drink. It will help you sleep."

"Sleep? First I must ask you to help me, Camillus. Help me. Talk to the doctors. What can I do with one leg? It is strange," he rambled on, "after we arrived in Naples I gave up the life of a soldier. I came north to my widowed sister. She has eight children and I worked as a painter of houses to help her. She has come to depend upon me. I gave up the old ways. I gave her money to keep the family together. I started going to church again and I have been as good as I could be, Camillus. See what the result is. I am to lose my leg, not in battle but because I fell from a ladder. Is it not a joke, Camillus? After all the battles I am at last wounded falling from a ladder."

"Life is strange, Albrecht. God works His ways."

"I cannot stand it," the man cried. "I do not believe it."

"We will see, my good friend."

Camillus persuaded Albrecht to drink and in a few minutes he fell into an uneasy sleep.

Camillus then knelt on the floor and taking the hot, limp hand of the sick man in his own he prayed intensely. "Oh Lord, make his trying hours that are so near as easy as possible. Do not let him suffer too much. He has always been a kind, just man, even if a rough soldier. Would that I could take on his suffering, for I have learned to love Thee and hope to suffer for Thee. Give me his burden of pain, Oh Lord. Spare my friend if it is according to Your plan."

Camillus felt waves and tremors of emotion grip him as he prayed through the long night. Occasionally the soldier roused and cried out, only to feel the soothing hands of Camillus and the quiet voice urging him back to the unknown, painless fields of sleep.

Finally, Camillus saw the early, gray light of morning touching the surgery, revealing the kind, distressed face of the young doctor who had summoned him the previous evening. "Maestro, I did not expect you to stay the night. This is indeed a great sacrifice."

Camillus stood up and smiled. "It was my privilege to stay with him. He is an old friend. I feel that the Lord has heard me and that the patient will not suffer too much. When is the operation?"

"Within the hour, Maestro."

"I should like to stay with him during his trial."

"It will not be pleasant."

"I know that. I have seen operations on the field of battle."

"We shall do our best for him."

"Camillus." Albrecht opened his eyes and to their astonishment was smiling.

"It is good to see you, my friend," Camillus said with forced heartiness.

"You have been here all during the night. Ah, you are a real comrade."

"I did not leave you, Albrecht. I do not intend to leave you."

"Ah, you remember Corfu, you rogue." Albrecht's voice was stronger and the doctor was looking at him closely.

"I remember many things and your kindness at Corfu is one of the most pleasant."

Albrecht laughed. "I was afraid to leave you." He turned to the doctor. "We all knew that nothing could kill Camillus de Lellis. I was afraid to leave him for fear that when he became well he would give me a sound thrashing."

The doctor noted the color in the face of the patient. "How do you feel today?" he asked, touching his hand to the other's brow.

"Strange, doctor," Albrecht said, a frown crossing his face. "I do not feel any pain. Have you already taken my leg?"

"No, not yet." The physician was puzzled.

"Well, get it over with," Albrecht said as calmly as if it meant nothing to him at all.

"Well spoken, like a true soldier," Camillus said.

"You will stay with me, Camillus?"

"I shall hold your hand, my friend. In a few days we will be sitting in the garden, drinking a little wine and talking over old times."

"Ah, I should like that." Albrecht closed his eyes.

"We shall give him something to drink. At least it will deaden the pain," the doctor said. "It is doubtful whether he will sleep through the operation. If he awakens you must hold him down for he will bolt against the straps."

Two doctors and two attendants entered. "One last look at the leg," the oldest physician said. "Then we will have him moved from the bed."

The other surgeon unrolled the bandages on Albrecht's leg and threw them into a container. He turned for inspection and suddenly grew rigid. His companions stared at the color draining from his face and then a fit of shaking possessed him.

"What is the matter?" Camillus asked, grasping him.

The physician shook his head and pointed to the bed. "I am all right. Look to him."

The other doctors bent over Albrecht and then, after an astounded silence, looked at each other.

"It is not possible."

"This is not the patient."

"Who is this man? Where is the one to be operated?"

"I tell you this is the man. The Maestro did not leave his side all night. Ask him."

The first doctor looked at Camillus. "This man does not even have a broken leg. His leg is completely well."

"I cannot believe it." The young doctor was trembling.

"Believe it. It is so. This man is completely cured."

"Praise be to Jesus Crucified!" Camillus suddenly cried out in his great voice as he fell to his knees. "Thank You, Oh Mightiest of All, Most Merciful God."

They all stared at the kneeling Maestro.

"This is a miracle," the old physician exclaimed and the two burly attendants crossed themselves and hastily left the room.

"A miracle at St. Giacomo," someone whispered.

Camillus rose to his feet, stared at the still silent and sleeping Albrecht and left the room, his heart aching with love and gratitude, his lips still moving in prayer.

"It is God's work and His alone," Philip Neri said at a consultation of the Guardians. "Thank Him all your days and pray for His servant, Camillus de Lellis."

He rejoined the doctors in the other room. "This must be kept as quiet as possible," he said. "The proper authorities shall learn of it and decide what must be done. For the present you must keep silent or the entire place would not have a bit of peace. All of the patients would be crying out for Camillus and God does not work that way."

"Father, what is your answer to this?"

Philip stared at the questioning faces. "There is no answer but God," he said. "Yes, that is the answer. God."

CHAPTER XVIII

"I have an idea." Some months later Camillus was taking Lodi and Norcino, his two closest confidants, into the plan he was formulating. "We will gather a few together in a group that will make the solemn promise to Christ to devote their utmost efforts to assisting His sick. We will make that our primary objective for His honor and glory. We can have certain rules, meet each day and discuss our problems, and pray for guidance."

"Where can we meet?" Norcino was practical.

"Yes, the authorities may not like the idea," Lodi agreed.

"Do not let that worry you. I have just the place to hold our gatherings. It is a spare room right here in the hospital. We will let it be known that anyone can join with us who proves that he is worthy and sincere. Our attention shall be directed at his efforts in caring for the sick. That will be the test. It is important that this band be made up of those who think first of Jesus Crucified."

Camillus now entered upon a new phase in his battle for the sick. He succeeded in gathering less than a half dozen about him who met and prayed each day before a large, carved Crucifix. Together they discussed ideas to better the frightful conditions in the hospital. The intense conviction of Camillus that he must follow his Beloved Crucified at all times and in all places and in all adversities was transferred to his followers.

A few months passed and then a peremptory summons to

the presence of Monseigneur Salvatti, ecclesiastical adviser to the hospital who had the final say in all matters, awakened Camillus to forces at work against him. He was ordered to discontinue the group. The hospital authorities, especially the clerical members including Philip Neri, deemed the organization a focal point for the dissatisfaction of those refused membership.

"You have gathered a small band about you, no more than five, comprised, I must admit, of the most conscientious men in the hospital. Is this true?"

"Yes, that is so, Monseigneur."

"Well, please explain why you have organized such a group. What is the precise idea?"

"We have resolved to follow Christ Crucified," Camillus declared with deep solemnity. "Our efforts and devotion are for Him. We intend to accomplish this by working through the sick."

"Camillus, I admire your ideals, your work, and what you have accomplished as Maestro De Casa. However, I cannot allow a special organization to exist within St. Giacomo Hospital."

"Allow?"

"That is the word. You have taken over a hospital room for your quarters, erected a crucifix and hold regular meetings. This must be stopped at once."

"Stopped? But I do not understand. It is God's work."

"You know that I have the authority to do what I have told you. This organization must be discontinued at once. Dismantle your meeting room and have no more of this society within the confines of this hospital."

Alone that night, Camillus knelt before the cross above his bed and lost himself in deep prayer until his head drooped and he fell asleep exhausted. A dream enveloped his mind, one that was to inspire him to additional determination. Long years afterward he referred to the influence of that night and claimed that the dream had been sent him from heaven to bolster his courage.

The crucifix appeared brighter and the figure leaned toward him and spoke clear words. "Do not be afraid, Oh man of small soul. Go ahead, for I will help you and be with you."

He awakened to find himself bathed in cold perspiration. The pale moon draped itself across the crucifix and lit up the patient, tortured head with a glorious aura. "God be praised," Camillus cried. "It is a great sign for me to carry on. Nothing now shall stop me from serving You, Oh Lord. Nothing, until I have accomplished Your will."

A knock sounded at the door and Camillus, with difficulty, came to his feet and opened it to look into an attendant's horror stricken eyes. The twitching lips emitted sounds that caused Camillus to cry out.

"What is the matter, Grazio? You are mumbling. Speak up."

The man was still in a stupor. "Come!" Camillus shook him. "Tell me the trouble."

"The plague!" The words rose to a shriek.

"What do you mean, the plague?" Camillus tightened his grip even while he felt the terrible import of the statement.

"It is right here in the hospital. There is a new admission at the back entrance. He has the plague!"

"Stop your nonsense." Camillus snatched his cloak from a chair. "There is nothing to fear. Come, show me."

They left the room and immediately the attendant turned and ran in the opposite direction. Camillus hurried as fast as he could toward the rear door, conscious of the severe, shooting pains in his leg. No one was in sight at the receiving room. Perplexed, Camillus opened the outside door and looked into the gathering gloom. Rain lashed his face and he saw a litter, a man bending over it, and a boy standing nearby with tears running down his face.

Bernadino Norcino turned toward him. "Good, it is you, Maestro."

"What is the trouble?"

"Oh, it is the plague," the other said calmly. "The two litter bearers who carried him here ran as soon as the doctor mentioned the word. It was that young and foolish Abronti who diagnosed him and then fled as quickly as the others. The boy is this man's son."

"Let us bring him inside."

"He will have to be carried. When the bearers dropped the litter they broke off the handles."

"That is an easy matter," Camillus said. "Bernadino, have the boy go in. There is a vacant room not far down the lower corridor with a bed in it. We will put this poor man there."

"Yes, Maestro."

"We must hurry." Camillus gathered the sick man in his arms as if he were a child. "Open the door, quickly."

"There, that is good," Camillus declared, when he had placed the man in the bed and Norcino had arranged the blankets, lighted a lamp, and had the boy sit in a far corner of the room.

Camillus opened a window, placing a screen before it. "Fresh air, but he must be kept warm." Camillus turned to the frightened boy. "Do not be afraid, little one. Your father will be well taken care of."

Bernadino was again examining the patient. "No doubt that it is the plague, Maestro. What shall we do now?"

"Bring water, cold water to drink and warm to bathe him. Get some disinfectant to wash this place completely. Go to the apothecary and tell him that I want some of that powder they claim has helped plague victims. We have it here for I ordered some. I want it in the correct quantities for dosages. Have him mark it well. If there is a doctor who will come, bring him. Hurry."

Bernadino left and Camillus busied himself stripping the clothes from the unconscious man and talking to the boy. "What is your name, little one? You need have no fear. We are here to help the sick and we will not run from your father. Remember, God is with us and we will rely upon Him. He will not fail us."

"I am Pietro Balzoni. He is my father. My two uncles brought him here but they did not know that he had the plague."

"So God will take care of him even if he has the plague. We will have something brought for you to eat. Do you feel sick at all?"

"No, no, Signor. I am well. And my sister is well, but my mother and the other children are in bed. When my father came home from work this night he fainted at the door and my uncles bore him here."

"Say prayers to Christ Crucified and the Blessed Mother." Camillus talked as he worked. "They will help. They never fail. Ah, here are our friends. Bernadino and Curzio, we are going to be busy."

"I have brought food for the boy." Curzio went over to the child.

"Good, take care of him. Ah, you have the drugs."

"There are six packets, one for every two hours."

Norcino assisted Camillus in bathing the feverish patient, then carefully covered him.

"What of the boy, Curzio?"

"He is not sick, Maestro, but very hungry."

"Take him to my quarters and let him sleep in my bed,"

Camillus ordered. "Return as quickly as possible and bring a lantern, more medicine, enough for at least a half dozen people. Put up a package of food. Boy, what is the address of your home?"

"Two doors left of the church on the Street of Closed Shops."

"We are going to see your family. You will wait here."

"God will reward you, Signor." The boy burst into tears.

Camillus patted the bowed head. "You must continue to pray, my boy. God will do what He sees fit and it will be for the best. Take charge of him, Curzio. Have you asked a priest to see this man?"

"I have told Father Profeta."

At that moment Bernadino returned with the goods ordered and with Father Proceta, one of the close friends of the Maestro. "The word has gone through the hospital and the servants are in panic," the priest said as he arranged the oils and cloths.

"They are stupid and cowardly," Camillus said. "When you return, Father, tell them that Bernadino, Curzio, and I will take care of this victim."

"They will not be anxious to come close to me," Father Proceta said.

"We have done what we could for his soul. His physical treatment has started and now Bernadino and I are going to this man's house. The family is sick and well may have the same illness."

"I shall stay here with Curzio," the priest said as he finished the administering of the oils.

"You are truly a priest of God."

Camillus threw on his cloak. When Curzio returned and reported the boy sleeping, Camillus and Bernadino, laden with their packages and lantern, went out into the night. Shortly they came to the Street of Closed Shops and had little difficulty locating their destination. A young girl stood before the door, crying.

Camillus gently patted the child's arm. "God has sent us to help you. We are from the hospital. Your father is resting, receiving the best of care. Your little brother is well. Why are you waiting here in this rain?"

"To beg the authorities not to make us leave," she said, "My uncles have left us and all who lived in the building have fled. They have nailed a red cross on our door and there has been talk of shipping us to the caves outside the city. We will all die if this is done. Oh, Blessed Mother, have pity."

"Ah, you have called upon the right one," said Camillus. "Where man's pity stops that of God and His Blessed Mother begins. You have been answered. What is your name, child?"

"Lucretia Balzoni, Signor."

"Lead us to your family, Lucretia."

They followed her up the rickety stairs of the old structure to the second landing where the rays of the lantern revealed a crude, red painted cross nailed to the door. "It is a good sign, this cross," Camillus said as the girl led them into a large apartment, comfortably furnished but pervaded with dampness. Two closed doors opened from the chamber.

Lucretia pointed to one of the portals. "My mother and the girls are in there. The boys are in the other room. They are all sick. I am very much afraid, Signor."

"God is here, my dear. Have no fear. Bernadino, light the fire and the lamps. Heat water, plenty of it." He beckoned to the girl. "Go, my dear, to your mother. You need have no fear."

"But the plague, Signor?"

"God will keep it from you. Hold my lantern while I light all the lamps. We shall have light, heat, and food as well as medicine for your family."

In the mother's room was a bed occupied by a woman and two small girls, all breathing heavily. Camillus blessed himself and bent over the bed for a quick examination. The marks of the plague were very apparent. He turned to Lucretia, who still trembled. "God may be willing to save them if you will do as I tell you, my dear."

"I will do just as you say, Signor."

"Then bring warm water from my friend. You must bathe your mother and sisters and dress them in clean, dry garments. You will then cover them with blankets. Each time I tell you you must give them medicine as I shall show you."

Camillus carefully mixed the powder and stirred the contents of each cup with great concentration. The girl helped him lift the patients in turn and Camillus gently but firmly forced the bitter smelling liquid into their mouths. "That is done, my dear. You see how easily we did it. Now you will bathe them. Keep cool cloths on their brows while I wash this whole place with disinfectant."

Camillus opened a small section of the window and went about the laborious business of washing every inch of the room. He prayed as he quietly but persistently went about his work throughout the long night.

It was not until the first pale splotches of light had carved the darkness of the skies that Camillus rejoined Norcino. His friend wiped his brow and sat down. "Maestro, I am finally tired."

"You are a brave and good man, Bernadino," Camillus said. "You must be grievously tired. You have washed everything in sight."

"Do you actually believe in this disinfectant?"

"It is advised, my friend. We know little about some things but common sense should tell us that cleanliness certainly helps."

"You had better have some hot soup."

"We must insist that the girl have something to eat."

"Always thinking of someone else."

Camillus smiled. "So, too, are you, my dear Bernadino."

"Lucretia," he called, and the child came from the inner room with such a look of joy upon her face that both men came to their feet. "What is this? You are happy, child?"

"My mother is awake and recognizes me."

"Praise be to God for He has done this," Camillus cried, running to the chamber. Not only the mother but the two girls were awake and three faintly smiling faces looked up at the giant.

Bernadino turned and left to return a minute later, a look of astonishment upon his countenance. "The boys are awake and full of spirits, Maestro. When I last gave them medicine two hours ago they were as still as sleeping lambs and now they are as frisky as new colts."

"Let us thank Christ Crucified and the Blessed Mother." Camillus knelt in the middle of the room and called upon God to hear his words of gratitude.

Within the hour a strange procession wound itself through the streets of Rome. Camillus and Norcino walked before a joyous crowd that shouted loud songs of praise. Both men walked slowly, holding small crucifixes aloft.

"Blessed be Camillus and his holy assistant."

"God be praised for this fearless man and his loyal follower."

"God has wrought a great miracle."

"The plague is conquered."

People stared from windows, balconies, and sidewalks.

"This is most embarrassing, Maestro," Bernadino muttered.

"No praise of God is embarrassing. These words are for Him, not us. He has performed a wonder this night."

From the hospital door Father Profeta, Curzio, and a group of hospital authorities, including Guardians and clergy, watched the approaching procession.

"Where is your patient?" Camillus asked as he saw Curzio.

"He is no more a patient." Curzio looked at him in awe. "He is well, cured, and has left but a few minutes ago to return home."

"He is cured of the plague," Father Profeta said softly.

"God be praised." Camillus knelt in the dust of the road and immediately all within view did the same.

CHAPTER XIX

Camillus now had another channel for his tremendous energy. Enrolled as a student at the Roma College of the Jesuit Fathers, he pursued his studies for the priesthood with the deep intensity that marked all his endeavors. He had decided to seek holy orders when he saw the need for priests to serve the sick. His position as Maestro De Casa and his wide range of friends among the clergy had gained him admission.

"I do not know how you attend to all your affairs," Father Proceta declared to him one night in the Maestro's office after he had completed some tutoring in Latin for Camillus. "You are not a well man, despite your natural strength and size. Your duties here are tripled because of your insistence on taking active part in caring for the patients and now you have taken up the burden of studies."

"God is always helping me. I do not have enough time, Father. I wish that the days were twice as long."

The Council of Trent had not yet put into law reforms concerning ecclesiastical education, so Camillus' course of study to reach the sacred priesthood still stood at two years. The time passed swiftly and at the end of it, thanks to the interests of his Jesuit teachers, he presented himself for his tonsure and minor orders. It was Bishop Goldwell, the only surviving English bishop of Mary Tudor's time, who administered the ceremony.

Camillus de Lellis was ordained subdeacon and deacon

during the Lent of 1854 and a priest on May 26, the Saturday after Pentecost. Fermo Calvi, Philip Neri, Father Proceta, Bernadino Norcino, Curzio Lodi, Virgilio Crescenzi who had assisted him in his studies, Philip Biazzi, and a few other close associates were on hand to receive Communion which the new priest distributed with deep humility and gentleness.

Another surprise awaited him. It was revealed by Philip Neri. "You have been appointed chaplain of the Church of the Madonna of the Miracles. The Guardians have asked me to tell you this, and your bishop has approved."

"Now my happiness is complete," Camillus said.

Camillus now took the only vacation he was ever to have from the sick. In company with Curzio Lodi he spent a brief time in the Abruzzi but was glad to return to the Eternal City and work. Back in Rome, they both went directly to the Church of the Madonna where Camillus had decided he would spend a great deal of his future time.

To their joy Bernadino Norcino awaited them. "I do not like to greet you with any news that is not pleasant," Bernadino said, "but you will learn what I am to tell sooner or later. There is much trouble at St. Giacomo. The word has gone around that you wish to resign as Maestro and spend your time with the sick in the city. You will receive much opposition. In fact I was allowed to leave with much reluctance on the part of the Guardians, especially when they knew I was heading for your church."

Camillus shook his head sadly. "Opposition to our proposed society for the care of the sick is strongest at St. Giacomo. As a priest I feel that the organization can be advanced to a point of recognition by the Church if we are not affiliated with any institution. They will receive a full explanation when I submit my resignation. I do not want to hurt anyone."

"We know what your aims are but they are not looked upon with friendly eyes," Norcino said.

"Well, I shall go in person within a few hours and have the whole matter settled."

The following day Camillus went to St. Giacomo and was warmly welcomed and escorted to the office of Monseigneur Cusano who had succeeded Salviatti as ecclesiastical head.

"Sit down, sit down," the prelate said, but Camillus soon noted a certain reticence in his manner. "It is indeed a great honor to have you back here, not only as Maestro but as a priest of God."

"Thank you very much. It is good of you to feel that way."

"Now what are your immediate plans? I know that you must have conceived some new ideas during your holiday."

"Well, yes, I have some ideas," Camillus said slowly. "I have decided to devote my time to my duties as chaplain at the Church of the Miracles. I am going to foster a band devoted to the care of the sick wherever they may be."

The other stared at him. "Indeed? Do you also intend to remain here at St. Giacomo?"

"I wish to spend my time in my church," Camillus replied. "I believe that our society will flourish faster if we are not connected with any hospital."

"If you insist upon doing this you will be working directly against the wishes of many of your best friends."

"It is God's work. I have been commanded to do this."

"God's work! God's work!" The Monseigneur was angry now. "You use this phrase to suit your own wild whim. Your idea is absurd. You can devote all of your time to the sick right here at St. Giacomo with all of the facilities necessary. There is no need to organize a band for this work."

"I am sorry, Monseigneur. I cannot agree. I cannot get the idea out of my head."

"It is because you do not wish to get it out of your head."
The official sat back and pointed his finger at the visitor.
"There is nothing more that I can talk to you about until
you have regained your senses. I will tell you this. I shall
do everything in my power to prevent you from making a
fool of yourself and your friends and destroying the welfare
of this hospital. You may go."

Camillus attempted to speak but was brushed aside. He
left the room in a greatly agitated frame of mind.

He had now reached the lowest point in spirits that he
could recall. His mental anguish was augmented by his
physical condition which had become progressively poorer.
The infection of his legs had penetrated deeply and the pain
was constant. Two large corns had appeared upon his feet
making walking extremely difficult while the iron truss about
his middle chafed and irritated. Sleep was at times impossible
and many long nights after Lodi and Norcino had retired
Camillus knelt in prayer before the crucifix.

"Suppose they are right and I am only stubborn," he cried
aloud. "Maybe God wishes me to remain at the hospital and
this idea of mine is madness after all. Oh Lord," he prayed,
"You, alone, can come to my aid."

He threw himself before the cross and was suddenly trans-
fixed. The ashen, tortured figure detached its arms from the
cross and extended them lovingly toward the prostrate giant.
The voice of God said to him, almost as before in what had
been a dream but was now stark reality, "Why distress yourself, O man of little soul? Go on with your enterprise, for
I will help you, seeing that this work is mine, not yours."

The vision given to Camillus was now the bulwark of a
determination that knew no bounds. Secure in his belief that
his work had divine assistance, he spared as little time as
possible for the functions necessary to live. All his efforts

were for the sick and his mind constantly turned over the problem of gaining recognition of his idea to create a society devoted exclusively to the ill.

The activities of the small group were transferred to the Hospital of Santo Spirito. His excuse that this institution was nearer to the Church of the Madonna of The Miracles was true but underlying it was the desire to avoid contact with the antagonism he had created at St. Giacomo. The strained relations were a sorrowful burden only lessened by the admonition received from his miraculous vision. He had not revealed the miracle to anyone but it served as a driving force.

The work at the Hospital of Santo Spirito was extremely difficult and under worse circumstances than those at his previous post. Camillus, himself, was responsible for much of the hardship for he had openly and many times insisted that he and his small band perform all the hardest tasks. Consequently, the other servants, finding certain patients too disgusting to be treated without qualms, coined a phrase that swiftly became popular with them: "Let us leave this to Camillus and his friends. They like it."

Life moved on in a set pattern for the little group at the Chapel of the Madonna. It became the center of activity for the whole section, and there were people constantly seeking aid. Camillus set up rooms to house those who needed immediate attention or a night's lodging and could not gain access to a hospital.

It was at this time that Camillus suffered a collapse that hospitalized him at St. Giacomo's for some weeks. Lodi and Norcino were also ordered to take rests. The strenuous labors, extreme poverty, and unhealthy environment of their abode had ended the first phase of their missionary work. It was this illness, however, that was the turning point in Camillus' career. Word of the collapse of the giant and his friends went the rounds of Rome. Admiration and praise flowed from all circles and his work became more publicized.

Philip Neri and Monseigneur Cusano surprised him by being frequent visitors at his bedside. Monseigneur Salviati and other officials at St. Giacomo also came to spend time with this man whom they all loved despite the foolish ideas they thought he possessed about the creation of a new religious order.

Convalescence was slow but as soon as he was able Camillus made excellent use of his time. He proceeded to write rules and set up a way of life for his little company. He often thought of his mother's dream in which she saw him leading a band of men with red crosses upon their capes. He resolved that such an insignia should be shown on the black cassocks of his dream organization. He prayed long to the Lord and asked that he might gain the blessing of the supreme ecclesiastical authority upon his society.

Eventually the three left St. Giacomo to go to a more suitable home made available through the generosity of certain friends. The additional financial burden of future payments on the property did not in the least bother Camillus whose faith in his divine master knew no limits.

Here hope blossomed for them in the presentation of new novices. The sight of these young men, their faces sincere and burning with the zeal he felt in his own heart, overcame De Lellis and he often burst into tears as he watched them at prayer. "God is good. He is fulfilling His promises," he said, and spent long hours of the night in deep prayer.

It was almost a miracle that the fame of this group should suddenly become a positive thing. Their zealous work and intense devotion to the neglected sick became known throughout the city and everywhere they were hailed with respect and reverence.

Camillus now felt that his work was along the right path but he appeared no nearer to recognition from the authorities. Consequently he spent even more time before the crucifix and never failed to rise with the firm conviction that all would be taken care of by his divine master.

It was at this time that he decided his band should also carry spiritual and physical comfort to those who were in prison. On one of these trips Camillus was led into a long, low, dark tunnel from which water dripped with monotonous dread. Necessarily stooping, he carefully followed in the jailer's steps, watchful where the yellow rays of the lantern fell on the slimy floor. It was here that he came face to face with his past life in an adventure that increased his fervent gratitude to God.

CHAPTER XX

"God help those that are here!" he cried. "How many are imprisoned in this hole?"

His guide was an indifferent man. Long association with the sufferings of the unfortunate had made him so and it was reflected in his voice and manner. "Only one is here, now, Father." Camillus thought he heard a chuckle and his blood tingled. "It is a waste of your charity to visit him. He is the worst of a bad lot. You know, Father, we have had as many as seven down here at one time but they don't last long. No, they don't last long."

"This is a foul place. It is the worst of a long line of bad prisons I have visited. Why must you keep human beings in a cellar like this? It is always cold, wet, and dark. Animals are treated better."

The jailer chuckled and the giant priest felt an urge to shake his merriment from him.

"These so-called men are worse than animals, Father. You could put them no place else. Only the most desperate are ever brought here. This breaks them, physically as well as mentally. It is for the good of the people. They deserve no better treatment, Father. Ah, here is the door of our only tenant."

They stopped before a heavily barred portal, the brass studs mildewed to a sickly green, a small opening gaping like a black mouth in the dull light.

"Hello. Hello in there." The jailer raised his voice.

The only answer was rustling as if of straw.

The guide turned his heavy face to the priest, a grin upon it. "Oh, this is a tough one, Father, stubborn and vicious. He is condemned to lose his head before the week is out."

"Why is he here? What unspeakable crime has he committed or could any man commit to be so imprisoned?" Camillus attempted to peer into the opening but could see nothing.

"He is a desperate highway robber who has not hesitated to murder a number of people outside the city. We were lucky to catch him. He was found asleep and sick two weeks past, recognized and seized. Oh, if he had been well we would not have had the chance."

"My sympathy is with him," Camillus said grimly. "Open the door."

"There was a time I would not dare," the jailer said, "but it does not matter now. He can hardly move and he has no weapons, just his vile tongue. You do good with many of these criminals, Father, but you will get no place with this one. Oh, he is a rogue, I tell you."

"Open the door, man," Camillus said, angered at the evident relish in the other's tones.

The door swung open with a creaking noise and the foul odor that escaped caused even Camillus to pause. He cast his lantern rays on a floor of rotting straw and saw a heap of rags in one corner. Crouched against the wet wall, eyes gleaming madly, was a ragged, emaciated, bearded man.

"You are in luck this day, Tiberio." The jailer affected a tone of joviality. "Here is a priest for you. He has brought you the chance to save your soul, but more important to you, hot soup and bread. What do you say to that?"

A whip lashed across the mind of the giant visitor. "Tiberio?" He echoed the name, staring at the shivering wretch. For a long moment they looked at each other in the faltering rays of the lantern.

"It — it cannot be." A rasping sound came from the prisoner. "No, no — but the height, the great height and that voice. I know you — I know you."

Camillus put his own light down and turned to the guide. "Put the lantern there on the floor and help me lift him."

"Lift him? Touch him? No, I cannot do that, Father. He is filled with vermin."

"I'll vermin you!" Camillus shouted, putting his iron grip on the jailer's shoulder.

"Ow, you are crushing my arm. You cannot do this to me."

"Quiet or I will do worse." Camillus gave the man a shove. "You do as I say or I will report you to the governor, but before I do that you will answer to me here and now. Yes, it would be better to lay this stave across your wretched back. Do as I say."

The frightened man stumbled forward as the prisoner staggered to his feet.

"Camillus de Lellis, it is you. I would know that temper any place. Many a time I have fled it." The wretch chuckled. "Camillus, it is your old friend, Tiberio. Oh, you are a smart one. You have come dressed like a priest to help me escape."

Camillus pushed the reluctant jailer against the wall. He felt the sting of tears as he embraced the shivering, babbling wretch. "You must sit on this bench." He guided his old comrade to the only piece of furniture. "Here." He stripped off his cloak and wrapped it about Tiberio. "Oh, I am glad to be with you, my dear, dear friend. How often I have prayed for you."

"You know this murderer?" the jailer asked as he brought forth the bucket of steaming soup.

"I'll take that, and watch your language," Camillus said

roughly, his arm still about Tiberio. He lowered him to the bench and sat beside him, the soup can balanced between his knees.

"Camillus."

"Say nothing, now, my friend. Eat first." He gently fed the wreck of his old companion. Gradually, Tiberio stopped shivering but Camillus did not release his arm.

The jailer, shifting from foot to foot, was filled with uneasy thoughts of what this strange priest might tell the governor. He dared not speak too freely for all the jailers of the city knew that this unusual cleric had high connections.

Tiberio was muttering, but little sense could be gathered from his mumbling.

"This man must be moved from this foul place," Camillus said.

"But this is where he has been sent."

"Do not question me!" The fierceness of the voice stopped the protest. "Prepare another place for him, a window with light and air or else I will go to your superiors inside the hour."

"Yes, yes of course, Father, but I am not at fault for his being here. I only follow orders." The man's voice faded as he disappeared with hasty step.

"My poor Tiberio," Camillus said as he tightened his arm about the prisoner.

"Yes, you are a priest. I remember now, Camillus. I thought I was mad when first I saw you but now I know. You are a priest," the wretched creature muttered.

"God has been good to me, Tiberio. He is good to you also, my friend. You must have faith and I will have you out of this hole in a very short time."

"No, I shall die here, Camillus. I am what I was called, a murderer, a thief, a man to be feared."

"No man is to be feared. We must fear only the Lord who loves us and then only for what we have done. Tiberio, you must feel sorrow for what you have told me."

"Yes, yes, Camillus. I am sorry for what I have done."

"That is sufficient. Now say no more until we have you out of this place." Camillus made the sign of the cross and said the words of absolution. Within a quarter of an hour the prisoner had been moved to a quiet room on an upper floor.

Camillus, to the astonishment of the jailer, bathed and then dressed the emaciated Tiberio in clean garments. "You must sleep now, my friend," he said. "I shall be back early in the morning with Communion."

"Communion. It has been a long time."

"The Lord does not count time," his friend said affectionately. He turned to the jailer. "You will see that he is cared for as best possible. I shall return very shortly."

"Of course, Father." The man was still amazed at what he had just seen.

Camillus spent most of that night in prayer and returned to the prison to find Tiberio much weaker. He administered Communion and stayed with his friend whose eyes never left him. Finally the patient slept and Camillus went about his work. When he returned a few hours later his old comrade had died. Camillus knelt by the bedside and prayed, a feeling of peace coming over him.

Later, facing his followers, now over fifteen in number, he told of his experience. "We must be certain that we miss no one on our rounds. It may be the one to whom God is sending us. Indifference on our part would be a grievous sin. There is one more request. I want all of you to pray that our order will receive the recognition of Holy Mother Church.

It is much needed. God has ordained it but it is up to us to accomplish it in His Name."

Camillus now faced the greatest of his struggles, the acceptance of his order as a definite part of the Church. The old pope had died and Sixtus V sat on the throne of Peter. Politics forbade the high authorities to intercede with the new pontiff until it was discovered what he was like. Camillus became used to refusals to co-operate in his quest.

"He is a man of great energy," one prominent church official stated. "He will be a great pontiff but we do not know him too well as yet. You had best wait and see how the wind blows."

"We do not know how the wind blows," Camillus said in exasperation. "Only God knows that and He knows that this is His work and not mine."

"Well, be that as it may. You can be sure that no cardinal or prelate attached to the Vatican will carry your burden to the pope at this time. This Sixtus comes from peasant stock. He can be very direct. Do you not know that as a boy he was a keeper of pigs?"

"Which means what?" Camillus cried, annoyed by high intrigue. "Keeper of pigs, keeper of men. I am not afraid, but I know that I must have intercession else I would go to the pope personally."

"That would be your great mistake. Can you not wait?"

"If God can wait then surely I can," Camillus muttered as he left, but his energies still persisted.

Another blow left De Lellis shaken. Bernadino Norcino, weakened under the terrible burden of work he carried, died in August and his friend was prostrated with grief.

Finally he gathered his band about him. "Why should we grieve?" he said. Bernadino has received what we are all looking forward to, the reward of the Lord. Now at last we have one who will really get the Lord to accomplish our aims. He is still working for us. Have courage, my children. God has again smiled upon us and our aims."

Recognition of the work of his little band was apparent whenever they walked the streets of the city. People cried out blessings upon them and followed their little procession with loud shouts of acclaim. No case was too terrible for the ministers to handle and the people of Rome became most fondly attached to them.

Still there was no opportunity for papal recognition and this was Camillus' goal. At the time of his greatest triumph before the common crowds the voice of the high Church kept silent. But Camillus, undaunted, remained firm in his intention.

CHAPTER XXI

Sixtus V was as yet unknown to many in authority and they hesitated to do anything that might incur his displeasure. His dynamic personality and positive authority had stunned the Romans, used to intrigue and equivocation. He spoke with finality and brooked no opposition.

Camillus refused to be discouraged but many a door was shut to him as soon as it was known that he was approaching.

In the midst of these discouraging journeys Curzio Lodi became sufficiently ill to be granted a leave of absence which was to extend to over two years.

Camillus was alone in his battle but never did he fail to tell all that he had the most powerful One on his side and that he would triumph. Affectionate but pitying remarks were often made about his mission. His physical ailments increased in intensity. At times he found them almost unbearable but he considered them blessings from the Lord. It was a grave task even to walk and he was forced to hobble with the use of a stick.

Uppermost in the mind of Camillus was the burning desire to have the aims of the society recognized as in union with the Church. For this he prayed incessantly and worked beyond human powers. It became habitual for him to take long walks about the city despite his physical disabilities which he offered up to God for the success of his mission. His one prayer was that the Lord would grant him a chance to have intercession with the Holy Father.

One day, discouraged by two failures that had promised success, he found himself in the outskirts of Rome in a neighborhood of fashionable and imposing structures. He paused to admire the beauty of a well-kept garden and suddenly thought he caught sight of a red biretta and cassock on the side porch of the house that boasted some magnificent floral adornments. He acted upon impulse and entered the gate.

Approaching the building he was conscious that the eyes of the man in the red biretta were upon him. He strode up the steps and dropped to his knee to kiss the ring that was automatically extended. Camillus then stood up and towered over the short, rather portly figure of a prince of the Church.

"This is indeed a surprise visit, Father."

"You must pardon this intrusion, Your Eminence. I could not pass when once I had sighted the red of your office. I am Camillus de Lellis, a humble servant of the Lord. Hear me, I entreat you."

"Ah, Camillus de Lellis. You are not unknown to me. I have heard many things, all good, regarding your work. I am happy to have you here."

"I do not even know your name, Your Eminence. Yet, notwithstanding this, I have a favor to ask of you."

"Most people do," the cardinal replied. "Well, this is a different approach. I am Cardinal Lauro. You are indeed a strange, young man but I know of your work and it is good. What is it that you have in mind?"

"Your Eminence is most kind," Camillus said. "I have come to implore your help, your assistance. I have a small group of devoted men with the principal idea of serving the Lord Jesus Christ through care of the sick. I seek the blessing and approbation of the supreme ecclesiastical authority. I have devoted much time to the thought of the organization.

I have the rules with me. Would you condescend to read them, to grant me a few minutes of your most valuable time?"

The cardinal smiled. "You have come prepared. You have the rules of this order with you. Oh, I am not too unfamiliar with your proposition. I have heard of it from many friends."

"I carry them with me at all times, Your Eminence. I have been seeking intercession with the Holy Father a long time but have been most unsuccessful."

The cardinal hesitated, then suddenly extended his hand. "I do not know why I do this, for I have been warned that I will be approached by you to see the Holy Father. Still your very earnestness urges me to listen to you. I know that you are sincere. Let me have those rules, young man. If they are found suitable I promise you that, because of your name — and also your temerity — I shall intercede with the pope in your behalf."

The cardinal was astounded by the sudden change in his visitor. Camillus fell on his knees and cried in a great voice that could be heard for some distance, "All praise to Christ Crucified. God believes in me. God bless you this day and forever, Your Eminence. You are fulfilling the Word of God given to me that my mission is His and will be successful."

"Well, well." The prince of the Church was taken aback. "It is good to see you so pleased and, yes, so positive." He thought for a moment. "Yes, I am glad that you saw me. I feel that I must do as you have asked. I shall not fail you. You shall hear from me."

"Shall I call upon you, Your Eminence?" Camillus asked eagerly.

"No, I shall communicate with you. I must warn you that you may have to exercise patience for it is not an easy matter to gain an interview with His Holiness. You must wait for me to call you."

"You shall be remembered in my prayers for the rest of my days, for you are the one who will unlock the door that has been shut to me. God be praised. May He continue to rain blessings upon your head, Your Eminence."

The cardinal was embarrassed by the intensity and profusion of the gratitude of this young giant and he backed away, waving his hand in friendly farewell.

All pain was now gone from Camillus. His whole being was suffused with joy that could not be concealed. On the way back to his friends he frequently shouted out praise to the Lord and called down blessings on the head of Cardinal Lauro. Pedestrians paused to stare at him. Some who did not know who the giant in the frayed black cassock was shook their heads in pity, but those who knew him smiled and some even echoed his words.

"God has delivered us," Camillus cried as soon as he had gathered his group together. "He has at last, in His own good time, beckoned us forward. God be praised. Let us all go to the chapel and thank Him from whom all good flows."

Camillus de Lellis sought to establish his society at a time when the popes of Rome had begun in earnest the offensive against hitherto victorious heresy. New religious orders were created for the most part as auxiliaries to fight for the supremacy of Holy Mother Church. Vigorous enforcement of the decrees of the Council of Trent and the establishment of colleges and seminaries to afford intensified education of the clergy were main objectives of the papacy.

Each day of delay brought further uneasiness. Cardinal Lauro sent brief messages but he explained that the procedure in the creation of a new order was a lengthy one. The day arrived when Camillus received word that his brief had been presented to the Holy Father and that he would hear more later. It was with tremendous impatience that he kept himself from haunting the palace of Cardinal Lauro but good sense restrained him. Even so, sometimes late at night, unknown to anyone, he watched the lights in the Cardinal's house go out one by one, hoping and praying that on the morrow he would have more news.

In time he was informed that he would be granted an audience with the Holy Father, the date as yet not stated. This only increased his intense excitement and his prayers. Meanwhile, the work of the band did not slacken and their charity and energy grew more famous.

Word now came to Camillus that the disposition of His Holiness was set down. The competent congregation could draw up the Brief of Approbation. In effect, the Rescript was issued March 18, 1586, and Camillus de Lellis was granted an immediate audience with Pope Sixtus.

A strange calm descended upon him as he entered the anteroom of the private chamber. There were many clerics, some richly garbed and others in severe monastic clothing, who looked with curiosity at the huge figure of the ascetic faced De Lellis. He had done his best to make his frayed cassock and cloak presentable but what was lacking in his apparel was more than compensated by the blazing light that came from his eyes and seemed to illumine his whole face.

At last he was admitted, to find Sixtus V surrounded by the ermine, red, and gold of many dignitaries. He prostrated himself at the feet of the Pontiff and in his great voice cried out his fidelity to the Chair of Peter and to Mother Church. Many of the aristocratic princes and those of lesser rank looked with astonishment upon the scene and raised their brows at the unorthodox voice of the giant.

Sixtus V, a sudden smile upon his face, rose, went forward, and personally helped Camillus to his feet. "You are what I have expected, my son," he said. "I am not disappointed in your address to me. It is apparent that you are the most sincere of men. There has been great and good news of your work, your completely unselfish devotion to the sick."

"Your Holiness, I am most grateful."

"Come," Sixtus said in gentle tones. "Tell me of your plans." He pointed to some papers in the hands of a nearby cleric. "Print does not tell all."

Camillus immediately poured out his innermost thoughts in a torrent of words.

"Ah, what vision you have," the Pope said. "It is indeed a holy work to minister to the poor and sick and unfortunate, to assist at the last hour on earth in making as many happy deaths as possible. It is a holy ambition. We are happy and pleased to give our blessing and approbation. In due time we shall have your congregation, as it grows, placed among the religious orders called Clerics Regular with the right to take the three solemn vows. For you and yours there shall also be a fourth vow, that of assisting the sick."

Camillus could contain his emotions no longer. Tears coursed down his gaunt features.

"Come, come, my son," Sixtus told him. "Think now. Is there no other grant we may make to your congregation?"

"Your kindness is beyond all other gifts," Camillus cried. "But yes, Your Holiness, there is one other. May we have the privilege of wearing a red cross on the breast of our habits and on the mantles, as a symbol of the love and sacrifice that animates us?"

"A noble thought, the Red Cross of the Lord," Sixtus said softly, his own spirit moved greatly at sight of this truly earnest petitioner. "It shall be granted as of this day and this cross shall mark your order from this hour."

The intense joy of Camillus and his band knew no bounds. When Camillus spoke to them his face was relieved of the terrific strain of worry. "We are, brothers, on the direct path to becoming an established order of Holy Mother Church. By your deeds, guided by the Lord, you have proved to the authorities that our work is the work of God. We are now in the process of being incorporated as an official order of the Church. God is pleased to entrust the treasure of charity to the sick into our hands. Yet, small as we now are, the day will come when we shall gird the world, when the red cross of our Savior shall spread thousands of miles. Sickness knows no bounds and henceforth our work will have no bounds. Truly, God is great and good."

He was lost in retrospection, his face bathed in a holy and tranquil light, his gaunt, giant frame a dignified assurance of power.

Not yet did he see the vision of plague ridden cities and hidden towns where epidemic ran rampant, confronted only by black cloaked, red cross shielded ministers. Yet faintly he thought he heard the cries and blessings of the millions that his order was to care for. In the far distance the whispering winds of the future breathed blessings upon his group. He could not see beyond the pall of time but he sensed the hospitals and houses of the order scattered around the band of earth.

The words of the soldier father he had loved so well came to him. "Your mother had a vision before you were born. It was that of you leading a great group of black robed men all with a red cross upon them, over their hearts. It is written that you will be a great soldier."

"Ah, Christ Crucified," he whispered, "make me always to be Your soldier, to fight for the victory You have given man over death."

EPILOGUE

For almost four hundred years the Order of Saint Camillus has circled the world with the Red Cross of its founder.

Today approximately 2000 members labor in thirteen provinces located in Italy, France, Germany, Spain, Austria, United States, Brazil, England-Ireland, Poland, Netherlands, South America, and China. The work of Saint Camillus is conducted in 86 houses, 47 hospitals of the order, 150 public hospitals.

The sick and the poor who have felt their aid number astonishing millions. Truly the words of Holy Scripture are the life motto of all Camillians: "What you did to the least of My brethren, you did unto Me."